Illuminati: The Conspiracy That Never Died

Allen Schery

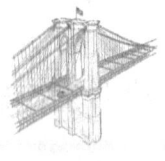

BROOKLYN BRIDGE BOOKS

Brooklyn Bridge Books

DEDICATION

I dedicate this book to my initial mentors in History. Though trained in Anthropology and Archeology, I never lost my interest in History. At Walt Whitman High School Romaine Francois Poirot and Alice D'Addario inspired my interest in History. At Post College Benjamin Ruekberg and Regis Courtemanche were fascinating characters who knew how to present History dramatically. All are now passed and will never know the effect they had. I send this dedication through the ether saluting their life essence.

Contents

Prologue
Unmasking the Illuminati.

In the shadowed corridors of history, whispers of hidden power echo through the ages. The name Illuminati stirs intrigue, fear, and endless speculation. Are they the masterminds behind revolutions, financial empires, and global influence? Or were they merely an intellectual society lost to time—victims of suppression, myth, and misinformation?

The truth is far more complex.

In the late 18th century, amid the Enlightenment's surge of radical thought and the crumbling structures of old authority, Adam Weishaupt founded the Bavarian Illuminati with a vision: a group dedicated to reason, philosophy, and the advancement of knowledge. Yet, secrecy bred suspicion, and rumors of a clandestine agenda quickly overshadowed their true intent. Were they seeking control? Manipulating governments? Or were they simply scholars navigating a volatile era?

Through centuries, their name has transcended reality, morphing into legend. From conspiracies of world domination to hidden symbolism in modern culture, the Illuminati have become the faceless puppeteers of countless theories. But where does history end and myth begin?

This book is not about indulgent paranoia or blind belief—it is a journey through time, meticulously peeling back the layers of fact and fiction. From their Enlightenment foundations to their alleged influence on revolutions, from suppression to resurgence in modern conspiracy lore, we explore the Illuminati as both historical actors and lasting myths.

Are they an extinct organization buried in archives, or a living force shaping the present? As we unravel their story, one question remains:

How much of the Illuminati is real—and how much is just shadows dancing on the wall?

Chapter One

The Enlightenment & Birth of Secret Societies – Setting the historical stage.

O n a cold, restless night in mid-to-late 18th-century Western and Central Europe, particularly in intellectual hubs like Paris, London, and the German states, behind shuttered windows and thick velvet drapes, a small group of intellectual rebels gathered in secrecy. In the hidden recesses of dimly lit basements and secluded salons, whispers of forbidden knowledge and subversive ideas wove through the darkness—ideas bold enough to shatter centuries-old dogmas and spark revolutions of thought and governance. These were not just vague notions; they encompassed ideas challenging the geocentric model of the universe, new philosophies advocating for popular sovereignty or individual natural rights over inherited power, emerging scientific materialism that questioned supernatural explanations, and an enduring fascination with esoteric or mystical traditions that promised hidden paths to spiritual truth and profound knowledge outside established religious institutions. Imagine the murmurs of brilliant minds—scientists, philosophers, and visionaries—exchanging coded messages about the power of reason and the possibility of a society liberated from tyranny. In these clandestine meetings, the seeds of modern democracy, unshackled inquiry, and radical intellectual networks were sown. It is where our journey begins: an immersive plunge into an era when reason dared to challenge absolute authority and secret societies were conceived as safe havens for revolutionary ideas that would shape the future of civilization.

For centuries before the Enlightenment reshaped Europe, life was governed by traditions that seemed immutable. Absolute monarchies ruled with unquestioned authority, their power sanctified by the doctrine of divine right, while the Catholic Church and other religious institutions permeated every aspect of daily existence. Learning and knowledge—whether sacred or secular—were the exclusive preserve of a select few: clergy, aristocrats, and academicians whose access to Enlightenment was tightly controlled by venerable institutions. While significant in their own right, the quality and rigor of pre-Enlightenment scholarship, such as scholasticism and early universities, operated within a different intellectual framework, heavily influenced by dogma. To question or defy this established order was fraught with peril, often inviting censorship, brutal suppression, and even death. This established order, however, had its fierce defenders, laying the groundwork for what would later be termed the Counter-Enlightenment. This persistent intellectual opposition sought to preserve tradition, religious authority, and social hierarchy against the radical individualism and rationalism championed by Enlightenment thinkers. These opposing forces created constant tension, profoundly influencing how clandestine groups operated and conceived their mission.

Nevertheless, deep political and ideological change undercurrents were stirring beneath this stable facade. The ravages of the Thirty Years' War (1618–1648) serve as a stark reminder: initially ignited by religious divisions, the conflict soon evolved into a struggle for political dominance, decimating vast regions of Europe. The Peace of Westphalia's aftermath introduced the radical notion of state sovereignty, challenging centuries of ecclesiastical and monarchical domination. In England, the English Civil War (1642–1651) pitted Royalists against Parliamentarians and culminated in the shocking execution of King Charles I in 1649—a powerful signal that even the divine right of kings was not infallible. With the later Glorious Revolution of 1688 replacing tyranny with constitutional monarchy and subsequent revolutions in America and France crystallizing Enlightenment ideals of liberty and equality, the old order was visibly crumbling, setting the stage for a radical reimagining of society.

Simultaneously, a transformation was underway in the realm of human knowledge. The Scientific Revolution, which began in the 16th century, dismantled the old cosmic order. No longer was the universe explained solely by ancient texts or dogmatic assertions. Empirical observation, controlled experimentation, and mathematical reasoning redefined the mode of inquiry. Copernicus's heliocentric theory, later vindicated by Galileo's telescopic revelations, shattered the entrenched geocentric model. Johannes Kepler's precise laws of planetary motion and Isaac Newton's unifying laws of physics revealed an elegant cosmos governed by immutable natural principles rather than capricious divine acts. Thinkers such as Francis Bacon, advocating the experimental method, and René Descartes, who famously declared, "Cogito, ergo sum" ("I think, therefore I am"), provided the intellectual apparatus for questioning established beliefs. Alongside these scientific luminaries, influential philosophers like John Locke challenged the very foundation of political authority by arguing for natural rights and a social contract; Voltaire's incisive wit and relentless criticism of oppression underscored the need for tolerance and reason; Montesquieu's analyses of governmental structure paved the way for modern ideas of separation of powers; and Rousseau's reflections on individual liberty and the social contract captured the yearning for equality. Their ideas, disseminated through widely circulated pamphlets and often debated in secret gatherings, offered a new model for understanding society based on evidence, reason, and the steadfast pursuit of truth. Nevertheless, the unbridled application of reason also presented its challenges, leading to internal debates among Enlightenment thinkers about its limits, its potential for social disruption, and, as critics would argue, its sometimes overly optimistic view of human perfectibility.

The transformative power of these ideas was dramatically amplified by another revolutionary invention: the printing press. Johannes Gutenberg's mid-15th-century innovation shattered the monopolistic grasp on handwritten texts, enabling the vast reproduction and rapid circulation of manuscripts, treatises, and pamphlets. Suddenly, classical literature, scientific discoveries, political essays, and radical ideas became accessible to a broader audience, fueling an unprecedented surge in literacy and public discourse. In coffee-houses and taverns, where printed material was passionately debated among diverse groups, the printing revolution democratized access to knowledge. It empowered dissidents and clandestine societies to disseminate their subversive ideas—even under the vigilant eyes of the authorities.

Amid these fermenting forces—political turmoil, scientific break-throughs, and the unleashed power of the printed word—secret societies emerged as vital sanctuaries for intellectual exchange and fearless debate. Directly born from the pervasive censorship and authoritarian control of the era, these organizations offered safe havens where revolutionaries could gather discreetly to reimagine society without the heavy hand of oppressive regimes.

Among the foremost of these clandestine groups were the Freemasons. Evolving from medieval guilds of stonemasons into an influential fraternity, the Freemasons embraced ideals of reason, philanthropy, and moral integrity. Their elaborate rituals, secret symbols, and layered hierarchies provided an internal language that fostered solidarity and allowed them to transmit their progressive ideals covertly. For many Enlightenment thinkers, Freemasonry offered a blueprint for creating a more egalitarian social order.

In parallel, the enigmatic Rosicrucians fascinated countless minds by blending mysticism, alchemy, and esoteric Christian thought into a quest for hidden wisdom. Publicized through mysterious manifestos such as the Fama Fraternitatis, they promised access to ancient, sacred truths and a deeper understanding that melded scientific inquiry with spiritual insight. To an era hungry for knowledge, the

Rosicrucian emphasis on secret wisdom was both tantalizing and emblematic of the drive to transcend the limitations imposed by tradition.

Not far removed in spirit, in the German states, a provocative yet humble society known as the Order of the Pug emerged in the mid-18th century. Formed primarily for Catholics excluded from mainstream Masonic lodges, this society adopted the playful symbol of the small dog. Through humor, mimicry, and satirical rituals, the Order of the Pug subtly critiqued the religious restrictions that stifled free expression, exemplifying how diverse responses to censorship could be both inventive and subversive.

At the same time, the Odd Fellows, first documented in England in 1730, pursued a distinctly communal path. Emphasizing mutual aid, social welfare, and personal development, they welcomed a broader cross-section of society. Their gatherings, which combined thoughtful debate with practical acts of charity, demonstrated that the spirit of Enlightenment was not solely the domain of intellectual elites but could be a collective endeavor towards a fairer society.

Among these varied groups, none would spark as enduring a legacy—and as much myth—as the Bavarian Illuminati. Founded in 1776 by Adam Weishaupt, a professor of canon law at the University of Ingolstadt, the Illuminati sought to advance the principles of reason, secularism, and intellectual emancipation, with an underlying, ambitious, perhaps even utopian, vision for re-engineering society from within. Far from the shadowy global cabal later depicted in conspiracy theories, the historical Illuminati were primarily dedicated to societal reformation through enlightened ideas. Their secretive operations, dictated by their time's hostile political and religious climate, eventually became entangled with embellishments that intertwined fact with rumor, reflecting the enduring human fascination with hidden power.

It is equally important to recognize that while these transformations were grounded in European history, their influence was not confined to the continent. Enlightenment ideas radiated outward, shaping intellectual currents around the globe. In North America, clandestine gatherings and the free circulation of printed ideas helped lay the ideological foundation for emerging democratic institutions. In Latin America—and even within regions of Asia and the Ottoman Empire—local intellectual movements absorbed and adapted these principles, interweaving them with indigenous traditions in struggles for independence. This global diffusion attests to the far-reaching impact of Enlightenment thought and reminds us that secret societies, too, were part of an international struggle for knowledge and freedom.

Another particularly vibrant facet of this intellectual era was the flourishing of salon culture. In cities like Paris, salons—often hosted by influential and well-connected women—became epicenters for literary and philosophical exchange. These gatherings opened private drawing rooms to a cosmopolitan mix of aristocrats, writers, and thinkers, blurring traditional social boundaries. The salonnières curated spirited debates on art, literature, science, and politics, providing a forum where ideas nurtured in secret circles and printed on pamphlets reached new audiences and deepened the impact of Enlightenment ideals on everyday life.

The literary world, too, played a subtle yet profound role in disseminating secret knowledge. Enlightenment literature—from essays and satires to novels and plays—wove allegories and encoded references to clandestine networks. Authors embedded within their works hints of society's inner workings and secret histories, lending an air of mystery to public discourse and ensuring that the debates sparked in hidden gatherings resonated on the printed page.

Adding further complexity is the internal diversity and factionalism within these secret societies. Far from being monolithic, many of these groups experienced internal debates, regional variations, and ideological splits. For example, while Freemasonry maintained a generally cohesive structure across Europe, individual lodges often reflected local political realities and social norms. Similarly, the Illuminati and Rosicrucians were not immune to internal discord—factionalism and varied interpretations of their founding principles contributed to their eventual dissolution or transformation, even as outsiders embraced a simplified narrative in their mythic allure.

However, as the revolutionary impulses of the Enlightenment spread, they also encountered passionate resistance—a movement often referred to as the Counter-Enlightenment. Reactionary thinkers such as Joseph de Maistre, Edmund Burke, and Johann Georg Hamann warned that unrestrained rationalism and relentless individualism could erode the social fabric and moral order. They championed the preservation of tradition, religious authority, and the wisdom inherited from the past, arguing that stability required a careful balance between progress and established norms. Their perspectives provided a necessary counterbalance to the radical ambitions of reformers and influenced how secret societies navigated constant threats from censorship and persecution.

The tapestry of this epoch is woven from many dynamic threads: violent political revolutions, groundbreaking scientific discoveries, the transformative power of the printing press, the cultured elegance of salon gatherings, and the covert operations of secret societies that sought refuge from oppression. In the majestic courts of kings and echoing halls of churches, the old regime once reigned supreme, yet in shadowed corners—from intimate salons to bustling coffeehouses—whispers of a radically new world began to circulate. Ideas became a potent currency of change, traded in hushed tones and boldly printed on pamphlets that dared to challenge centuries of orthodoxy. Secret societies emerged as conspiracies and vital sanctuaries for those who envisioned a future defined by reason, equality, and justice.

Today, as we survey this tumultuous epoch, it is crucial to disentangle the rigorously documented origins of these secret societies from the myths that later enshrouded them. Archival records and contemporary accounts witness the pivotal contributions of the Freemasons, Rosicrucians, Odd Fellows, salons, and the Illuminati in disseminating Enlightenment ideals. Nevertheless, rumor mingled with fact over time, and legend merged with history—transforming these narratives into enduring folklore that continues to captivate our collective imagination.

This comprehensive panorama—from the old regime of divine authority and relentless political strife through the seismic innovations of science and print to the nurturing grounds of clandestine gatherings and secret societies—provides a robust foundation for understanding the genesis of modern democracy and rationality. It also explains why, centuries later, the allure of secrecy, the quest for hidden knowledge, and the magnetic pull of mysterious power continue to mystify us. As we move forward in this exploration, we are invited to ponder: What truly separates documented history from the myths that have grown around it? The journey into the hidden corridors of power, reason, and clandestine society begins here and promises to reveal a legacy as complex as it is enduring.

Chapter Two
The Founding of the Bavarian Illuminati (1776) – How Adam Weishaupt created the group.

Before the clarion call of reason and critical inquiry shattered the long-held chains of medieval authority, Europe existed in a state of near-perpetual twilight. For centuries, truth had been dictated by tradition, divine right, and the decrees of the Church. Society was arranged in an almost unyielding stratification, with knowledge reserved as the exclusive province of a privileged few. The ordinary people—kept in the dark by institutions steeped in superstition and enforced obedience—had little opportunity for independent thought. Nevertheless, beneath this heavy veil of repression, whispered dissent began to swell in clandestine gatherings: secret meetings in dim back rooms, quiet conversations along narrow cobblestone alleys, and discreet debates within the private salons of influential households. It is from this charged atmosphere of suppressed potential that Adam Weishaupt emerged, setting in motion an experiment in covert reform that would eventually alter the landscape of intellectual resistance.

Born in 1748 in the scholarly town of Ingolstadt, Weishaupt was immersed in a Jesuit-controlled education that prized ritual, obedience, and orthodoxy over inquisitiveness. Indeed, the rigor and hierarchical structure of his Jesuit training, which emphasized discipline and systematic instruction, ironically provided a blueprint for the clandestine organization he would later build, even as he sought to subvert the ideology it promoted. His keen intellect and restless curiosity challenged these rigid strictures even as a youth. As his studies progressed and the revolutionary ideas of the Enlightenment began to permeate European thought, Weishaupt's perspective shifted from passive acceptance to active questioning of authority. Drawing inspiration from the writings of John Locke, Voltaire, Rousseau, and Montesquieu, his early essays—later collected under titles such as On Materialism and Idealism—reveal a gradual yet profound transformation. Though not widely disseminated at the time, these early philosophical inquiries clearly laid the groundwork for his later organizational efforts. While Weishaupt's path diverged radically from traditional dogma, his intellectual evolution was part of a broader, albeit often contentious, trend within European Catholicism where some clergy and scholars sought to integrate Enlightenment ideals with religious thought, a phenomenon sometimes termed the "Enlightenment Jesuits." In one memorable passage, he declared, "The light of reason must be kindled in the heart of every man if he is to break the chains of blind obedience," a conviction that would define his life's work. This formative intellectual awakening isolated him from traditional thinkers and prepared him to become a beacon for a generation seeking liberation from dogmatic control.

By the time Weishaupt assumed his position as a professor of canon law at the University of Ingolstadt, his convictions had crystallized into a bold and daring mission. His public lectures, imbued with Enlightenment philosophy, began to subtly—and eventually more openly—challenge the Church's and the aristocracy's authority. A small circle of like-minded students and disenchanted colleagues gathered, drawn by his passionate questioning of established power. Aware that open dissent in an era of harsh repression was tantamount to heresy, Weishaupt resolved to work away from the public eye. Thus, on May 1, 1776, at 28, he founded the Bund der Perfektibilis-ten (Covenant of Perfectibility), deliberately evoking the idea that humanity, through disciplined and rational effort, possessed a latent potential for moral and intellectual self-improvement and societal advancement, a perfection not granted by divine grace but achieved through human endeavor. This society's founding represented a quiet yet determined defiance—a promise to nurture change from the inside out. This endeavor, however, was fraught with immense practical challenges, as establishing and maintaining covert networks in an age of pervasive surveillance and severe penalties for dissent was a precarious undertaking, making Weishaupt's early successes all the more remarkable.

Not long after its inception, the society underwent a symbolic transformation that deepened its philosophical resonance. Embracing the name Illuminatenorden—the Order of Illuminati—the group signified its mission to dispel the darkness of ignorance with the radiant glow of reason. In a dramatic act of personal reinvention, Weishaupt assumed the clandestine pseudonym "Brother Spartacus," evoking the legendary rebel who had once defied tyrannical forces. This deliberate choice redefined his public persona and underscored the society's dual objective: to foster profound internal transformation and methodically infiltrate established institutions. Using secret names and encrypted communications imbued the group with a mystique that bonded its members and shielded its operations from prying eyes. These elements cultivated an internal mythology that inspired loyalty and secrecy.

Central to the Illuminati's operation was the ingenious hierarchical structure Weishaupt devised, which married the Enlightenment's call for discipline with the strategic imperatives of covert reform. Drawing on the ritualistic traditions of Freemasonry and academic fraternities, he established a tiered system beginning with the Novice level, advancing to the rank of Minerval, and ultimately culminating in the inner circle known as the Areopagus. Each step was marked by elaborate initiation ceremonies that featured symbolic recitations, allegorical rituals, and the display of cryptic emblems. For instance, new initiates took solemn oaths while facing images such as the "all-seeing eye" and intricate geometric patterns designed to suggest order, clarity, and the promise of Enlightenment. These rites served multiple functions: they strengthened internal cohesion, underscored the significance of personal sacrifice, and ensured that every member remained committed to the collective pursuit of reason. Such rituals, layered in symbolism and tradition, became a daily reminder that the journey toward intellectual liberation demanded personal rigor and shared resolve.

Beyond establishing internal order, the Illuminati developed a comprehensive strategy to influence the broader social and political landscape. Weishaupt envisioned his secret society as a long-term catalyst for change—a tool to gradually infiltrate and reform key institutions such as the government, academia, and even circles of the aristocracy. Members were carefully chosen and recruited from these influential sectors, with the explicit intent of planting the seeds of Enlightenment thought into the heart of power. In clandestine meetings, where vigor, debate, and ritualistic exercises merged, the members exchanged encrypted messages and symbolic gestures that cemented their dedication to reform. These gatherings were intellectual symposiums and operational hubs where strategic plans were crafted in absolute secrecy. By choosing a path of covert infiltration rather than overt revolution, the Illuminati believed that true, lasting societal reform could be achieved gradually—quietly altering the foundations of established order from within.

Modern scholarship continues to analyze the Illuminati's operational methods and symbolic language, often marveling at the ingenious blend of rationality and mysticism. Detailed records—fragmentary due to the society is inherently secretive nature—confirm that symbols such as the "Eye of Providence" and recurring numerological motifs were chosen for their layered meanings. Weishaupt's writings further illuminate his belief that "illumination of the mind through symbolism is the cornerstone of awakening," a notion that still provokes extensive academic debate. Interactions between the Illuminati and other contemporary secret societies, including various Masonic lodges and esoteric orders like the Golden and Rosy Cross, reveal a vibrant cross-pollination of ideas during the late Enlightenment. These interactions not only enriched the intellectual fabric of the time but also ensured that the revolutionary concepts pioneered by the Illuminati would influence subsequent reform movements for generations to come.

Inevitably, as the Illuminati expanded its ranks and diversified its membership, the conservative Bavarian authorities began to take notice. Determined to preserve the longstanding balance between Church and state, officials launched a vigorous campaign to root out any covert organizations that might challenge the order. Starting in the mid-1780s, systematic investigations, decrees, and arrests ensued. Many key figures were forced into hiding or exiled, and a significant portion of the society's records were either confiscated or deliberately destroyed. Although the public existence of the Illuminati was suppressed by 1785, the ideological and symbolic legacy of Weishaupt's creation persisted—fueling both scholarly inquiry and enduring cultural mythologies that captivate imaginations even today.

Contemporary historians remain divided regarding the long-term impact of Weishaupt's experiment. Some, such as Jonathan Israel, argue that the Illuminati's relatively brief lifespan limited its direct influence on European politics. Others, including scholars like Peter Gay and contributors to H-Net discussions, assert that the Illuminati's innovative organizational tactics and intellectual provocations had a lasting impact on the development of modern secret societies and reform movements. Emerging analyses based on recently uncovered correspondence and newly interpreted ritual texts enrich our understanding, ensuring that debates about Weishaupt's legacy remain vibrant and nuanced.

In retrospect, the founding of the Bavarian Illuminati is a sweeping testament to Adam Weishaupt's visionary genius and unwavering commitment to Enlightenment ideals. His daring experiment—merging rigorous intellectual inquiry with a meticulously structured secret organization—demonstrates that profound social change need not erupt solely from overt revolution. Instead, transformation can occur quietly through established institutions' gradual infiltration and reconditioning. The legacy of the Illuminati, woven through layers of encoded symbols, ritualized ceremonies, and strategic subterfuge, endures as a powerful emblem of resistance against oppression and a call to seek the light of reason continually.

Ultimately, the story of the Bavarian Illuminati transcends its status as a mere historical footnote, evolving into a complex narrative of ambition, ideology, and perseverance. Adam Weishaupt's creation is not simply an artifact of the past; it is a living reminder that the fusion of intellectual brilliance with strategic covert operations can challenge even the most deep-seated power structures. Illuminati's enduring influence on later secret societies, reform movements, and even modern conspiracy theories speaks to the timeless appeal of their vision. This vision inspires new generations to question authority, champion intellectual freedom, and relentlessly pursue the transformative power of truth.

Chapter Three

The Intellectual Foundation of the Illuminati – The Thinkers Who Shaped Their Philosophy

B efore the clarion call of reason and critical inquiry, Europe was a realm of boundless darkness—an era when truth was dictated solely by ancient dogma and the unchallenged authority of kings and clergy. In those shadowed days, society was defined by rigid hierarchies and the unquestioned tenets of superstition. Most people lived under the suffocating weight of an inherited order where divine right and ritual governed every aspect of life. Knowledge was hoarded by a privileged few in venerable institutions, and independent thought was dangerous; doubt was swiftly silenced, and the spark of human potential lay smothered by the insistence on conformity. Nevertheless, even in that oppressive gloom, the first daring whispers of rebellion began to stir. A revolutionary vision took shape in secret discussions behind closed doors—whether in narrow cobblestone alleys or lavish, candlelit salons. This nascent hope promised that one day, reason, empirical inquiry, and the belief in inalienable human rights would shatter the chains of ignorance and tyranny, heralding a new age of enlightened debate and progress.

Within this transformative context, the Illuminati forged its intellectual foundation. Emerging from the same embers igniting modern democratic thought, an extraordinary group of thinkers redefined politics, science, and culture. Their ideas were not merely abstract musings but practical blueprints designed to challenge authority and rebuild society on the pillars of reason and equality.

John Locke was at the forefront of this intellectual revolution. In his Two Treatises of Government, Locke rejected the long-held doctrine of the divine right of kings and argued that legitimate government must arise from a social contract formed through the consent of the governed. His assertion that everyone is endowed with immutable rights—to life, liberty, and property—provided an audacious moral framework that undercut centuries of authoritarian rule. For the reformers meeting in clandestine quarters, Locke's principles represented the possibility of a society where power was reimagined as a mutual responsibility, grounded in rational debate rather than inherited privilege.

Complementing Locke's revolutionary political philosophy was the acerbic brilliance of Voltaire. Through biting satires and trenchant essays—exemplified by works like Candide—Voltaire attacked the Church's and the state's abuses, decrying the institutional intolerance that had long suppressed free inquiry. His calls for civil liberties, freedom of speech, and religious tolerance resonated with those who dared to think independently, setting the stage for a new era in which truth could be reached by questioning authority rather than accepting it uncritically.

Jean-Jacques Rousseau further deepened this vision by reimagining the very nature of the political community. In The Social Contract, Rousseau contended that political legitimacy arises only when citizens jointly form and abide by collective will, which he termed the general will. His stirring argument for direct democracy and social equality offered secret reformers an ideal of participation that bypassed traditional hierarchies. Rousseau's potent and challenging vision served as both inspiration and a call to action for those determined to dismantle the oppressive structures of their time.

Montesquieu contributed another crucial element with his rigorous analysis in The Spirit of the Laws, advocating for the separation of governmental powers. His methodical division of authority—into legislative, executive, and judicial branches—offered a clear strategy for preventing the concentration and abuse of power. Secret societies drew on Montesquieu's insights to craft internal organizational structures that balanced leadership and accountability. Such models provided a tangible mirror to the reformers' ambitions: a system of checks and balances in public governance and within the secretive networks themselves.

While political doctrines radically transformed, the natural sciences were experiencing their revolution. In Novum Organum, Francis Bacon championed the experimental method and insisted that knowledge should derive from systematic observation rather than ancient texts. His call for an empirical approach laid the groundwork for a new understanding of truth—a belief that every fact of the natural world could be uncovered through rigorous investigation. This commitment to empirical inquiry deeply influenced reformers, who saw in Bacon's methods a means to question every presupposition of the old order.

René Descartes, with his declaration "Cogito, ergo sum" ("I think, therefore I am"), turned inward to place human reason at the center of all inquiry. His method of systematic doubt, urging individuals to discard any belief that could not withstand rigorous scrutiny, became a hallmark of modern philosophical thought. For the members of secret societies, Descartes' insistence on the primacy of reason was both inspirational and practical—a tool by which they rebuilt their worldview from the ground up. While Bacon emphasized empirical induction and Descartes's rational deduction, these two fundamental approaches underscored the diverse, sometimes even conflicting, paths to truth explored by Enlightenment thinkers, each striving to dismantle reliance on dogma.

These groundbreaking ideas found collective expression in one of the era's most ambitious projects: the Encyclopédie of Denis Diderot and Jean le Rond d'Alembert. More than a mere compendium, the Encyclopédie was a manifesto—a bold declaration that knowledge, once confined to the privileged elite, must be liberated. Its many pages, filled with the latest scientific discoveries and philosophical debates, provided tangible evidence that the power of educated discourse could smash the walls of ignorance. Its volumes circulated widely in clandestine circles, reinforcing the conviction that spreading information was key to overturning oppressive regimes.

The vibrant salon culture flourishing in cities like Paris was integral to the diffusion of these radical ideas. In opulent drawing rooms hosted by influential women and enlightened aristocrats, spirited debates on art, literature, and philosophy broke down long-standing barriers of class and privilege. In these intimate assemblies, ideas were refined through vigorous debate, and lifelong bonds were forged among those united in the cause of progress. The salons nurtured new ways of thinking and provided the networks that secret societies would later harness. Beyond political and scientific realms, the Enlightenment also saw burgeoning economic philosophies, such as those of the Physiocrats, who sought to apply natural laws to societal wealth and challenged established mercantilist practices, further expanding the scope of rational inquiry.

Nevertheless, perhaps the most fascinating aspect of this intellectual upheaval was its translation into actionable methods—the practical ways in which Enlightenment philosophy was embedded into the operational fabric of secret societies like the Illuminati. The structure of the Illuminati itself became a reflection of these Enlightenment principles. Drawing inspiration from Freemasonry's disciplined rituals and coded communications, Adam Weishaupt, the founder of the Bavarian Illuminati, devised an intricate hierarchical system. Membership was organized into clearly defined levels—from Novice to Minerval and ultimately to the inner circle of the Areopagus—with each stage marked by rigorous initiation ceremonies designed to foster moral and intellectual refinement. Members adopted pseudonyms to protect their identities, ensuring the secrecy necessary for free and fearless debate in an age of repressive oversight.

Using symbols and coded language was another practical adaptation of these revolutionary ideas. Just as Descartes and Bacon employed the language of skepticism to challenge inherited narratives, the Illuminati crafted their lexicon—replete with ciphers, emblems, and ritualistic practices. Their carefully chosen symbols—frequently invoking imagery of "light" or an "eye"—were not merely ornamental; they were expressions of the core Enlightenment commitment to illumination through knowledge. In these symbols, the pursuit of truth was poetically likened to stepping from darkness into clarity.

These structural innovations enabled the Illuminati to infiltrate and influence broader societal institutions covertly. Weishaupt envisioned the order as a catalyst for gradual, enlightened reform—a network that would educate its members, instill moral virtue, and disseminate advanced ideas throughout society. Their secret meetings were more than casual gatherings; they were meticulously orchestrated sessions in which intellectual debates were paired with rigorous rituals designed to inspire self-discipline and unwavering loyalty to the cause. The emphasis on moral and intellectual perfection was not an abstract ideal but a practical guideline for daily life, subtly reshaping the institutions around them.

Later figures such as David Hume and Immanuel Kant refined these transformative ideas as the Enlightenment advanced. Hume's empirical skepticism questioned the notion of causation and diminished the blind reverence for tradition. In contrast, Kant's stirring appeal to "dare to know" (Sapere Aude) challenged each individual to exercise reason independently and helped create a resilient moral framework against the forces of dogma. Their contributions deepened the intellectual rigor of the movement. They established that continuous self-examination was essential to progress—a doctrine adopted wholeheartedly by secret societies committed to perpetual reformation.

Into this rich tapestry stepped Adam Weishaupt, whose vision embodied these interwoven ideas in practical form. Educated in the radical philosophies of his time and deeply influenced by the fervor of salon debates and the revolutionary power of printed knowledge, Weishaupt sought to create a covert organization that would serve as a living laboratory for Enlightenment-inspired reform. For him and his collaborators, the formation of the Illuminati was not a mere conspiracy but an audacious strategy to rebuild society from within—using hierarchical methods, symbolic rituals, and coded communications to challenge every form of tyranny, whether ecclesiastical or monarchical.

Thus, the intellectual foundation of the Illuminati is a vast tapestry woven from the threads of Enlightenment thought. It is composed of the radical political theories of Locke, the incisive critiques of Voltaire, the egalitarian visions of Rousseau, and the systematic organizational ideas of Montesquieu. Bacon and Descartes redefined the methods by which knowledge was acquired, while Diderot, d'Alembert, Hume, and Kant ensured that this new doctrine was as resilient as it was revolutionary. Their influence did not remain confined to abstract treatises or academic debates; it manifested in the practical, day-to-day operations, symbols, and rituals of secret societies striving to reconstruct an oppressive world based on reason and justice.

In its final analysis, this transformation was nothing short of revolutionary. The old world, marked by rigid obedience and dogmatic control, yielded to a vibrant new order—a world where reason could illuminate even the darkest corners of society. The legacy of these great thinkers endures as a testament to the power of ideas to reshape civilization. Their influence, nurtured in the intimate enclaves of salon debates and covert, ritualistic gatherings, paved the way for the birth of secret societies like Illuminati and laid the groundwork for modern democratic institutions built on equality, justice, and perpetual inquiry.

Chapter Four

The Role of Freemasonry & Other Secret Societies – Connections between the Illuminati and other groups fueling speculation.

I n the heart of the Enlightenment, when the rigid structures of church and state were under fierce intellectual assault, secret societies emerged as sanctuaries of liberated thought and instruments of covert political transformation. Among these, the Freemasons and the Illuminati have come to embody the twin paradoxes of light and shadow—one evolving gradually from medieval operative guilds into a global fraternity dedicated to ethical self-improvement and charity, and the other founded in 1776 by Adam Weishaupt as a focused, subversive tool for dismantling entrenched power structures. Over the centuries, these groups have shared a language of symbols, rituals, and coded communications that has left a historical imprint and fueled persistent speculation about a unified network of hidden influences.

Freemasonry, with its origins in the stonemasons' guilds of medieval Europe, developed over time into a vast international organization characterized by its hierarchical system of degrees, ritualistic initiations, and emblematic iconography such as the square, compass, and the all-seeing eye. This broader movement, encompassing diverse rites and national Grand Lodges, often displayed regional variations in focus and interpretation but maintained core tenets of brotherhood and moral uplift. Early ritual manuals and constitutions—many dating back to the early eighteenth century—reveal a carefully constructed progression through degrees (Entered Apprentice, Fellowcraft, and Master Mason) designed to instill moral lessons and elevate personal virtue. These symbols and ceremonies were not merely abstract; they were public markers of a brotherhood committed to creating a better society through mutual support, philanthropy, and ethical conduct, often promoting Enlightenment ideals of reason, tolerance, and scientific inquiry within their lodges. Documents now housed in various Masonic archives bear testimony to these traditions, and extensive printed materials from the period underscore both the aesthetic and functional aspects of Masonic lore. Despite their stated aims of benevolence, however, Freemasonic lodges often faced suspicion from entrenched religious and monarchical authorities, who viewed any independent association outside state control as a potential threat, even before the more radical Illuminati emerged.

In contrast, the Illuminati were born out of a deliberate rebellion against the religious and aristocratic hegemony of late-18th-century Bavaria. Disillusioned by the abuses of institutional power, Adam Weishaupt envisioned an order that would use secrecy to infiltrate and ultimately subvert the established order. Drawing deliberately and strategically on established forms, Weishaupt structured his society with initiations and hierarchies that echoed Masonic traditions yet repurposed these rituals for a radical agenda. This calculated emulation not only provided a veneer of familiarity but also allowed for infiltration and the recruitment of disaffected Masons. Primary source evidence—which includes fragments of the Apologie der Illuminaten, letters preserved in European archives, and contemporary reports—demonstrates that Illuminati initiations involved allegorical recitations, oaths denouncing blind obedience, and the adoption of symbols like the "all-seeing eye" to represent the pursuit of enlightened knowledge. This deliberate emulation of the Masonic ritual provided protection and immediate credibility within circles that revered secrecy and symbolism.

A wealth of archival research reveals that overlapping memberships were common in Enlightenment Europe. Prominent intellectuals and reformers, driven by the lure of hidden knowledge, frequently joined Freemasonic lodges and the nascent circles of the Illuminati. Figures such as Freiherr von Knigge—whose name appears in both Masonic registers and Illuminati documents—are prime examples of how these affiliations reflected more an era's cultural appetite for secret societies rather than evidence of a deliberately unified network. Such dual memberships frequently stemmed from shared social circles and a general intellectual curiosity among reformers rather than a deeper ideological merger of the distinct organizational goals of the two groups. Scholars have analyzed personal correspondences, lodge minutes, and recruitment records, noting that many members sought access to both groups' intellectual capital and social influence. While later conspiracy theorists have seized upon such dual memberships as incontrovertible proof of an all-powerful cabal, rigorous historical scholarship consistently points to individual ambition and the drive for social advancement as the true motivators behind these overlapping affiliations.

The political and social pressures of the time played a crucial role in how these secret societies developed—and how they were later repressed. In states like Bavaria, where the authorities were unwilling to tolerate dissent, extensive state-sanctioned investigations were launched to root out any organization perceived as subversive. Such repressive measures, however, were not unique to Bavaria; similar crackdowns, driven by monarchical and religious anxieties, occurred across various European nations, contributing to a continent-wide climate of suspicion towards clandestine groups. This climate was further exacerbated by a burgeoning body of anti-Masonic literature, which, even prior to the Illuminati's public exposure, frequently speculated about the hidden political agendas and interconnectedness of secret societies, inadvertently laying groundwork for later conspiracy theories. Official decrees, as documented in state archives, led to the confiscation of Illuminati manuscripts and even the exile of key members during the mid-1780s. Such repressive measures, recorded in governmental reports and ministerial correspondences, contributed to gaps in the historical record that later fueled myths of a vast and impenetrable underground network. The deliberate suppression of documentation only intensified the mystery around these groups, inviting public speculation that blended fact with imaginative exaggeration.

As the Enlightenment advanced, a shared cultural vocabulary emerged—one in which secret symbolism was nearly ubiquitous. The all-seeing eye, for instance, appears in Masonic lodge decorations, illuminated manuscripts, and even later on national emblems and currency. Detailed iconographic studies, such as those published in academic journals and reference works on symbolism (for example, in Springer's reference entries on secrecy), trace the origins of these images to ancient civilizations, highlighting their evolution over time. While in Freemasonry, the symbols were explicitly tied to moral instruction and the promotion of virtue, in the Illuminati, they were recontextualized as emblems of resistance against oppressive authority. This duality is frequently cited in scholarly debates, with historians such as Jonathan Israel and Peter Gay arguing that such symbols reflect the broader cultural heritage of the Enlightenment rather than any coordinated effort for conspiratorial control.

Beyond these two groups, other esoteric orders contributed additional layers of complexity to the cultural landscape. The Rosicrucians, whose allegorical texts and secret rituals traced back to mystical traditions within Europe, and the revived Knights Templar, replete with chivalric symbolism and clandestine meetings, adopted iconographic elements that resonated with both the Illuminati and Freemasonry. Comprehensive studies of secret societies—such as those found in academic publications and ethnographic research on fraternity cultures in America—demonstrate that the widespread use of overlapping motifs was a natural outcome of the era's intense interest in hidden knowledge, reflecting a convergent cultural evolution in symbolic language. These symbols, passed down and adapted over multiple centuries, became the staple language of mystique that modern conspiracy theorists would later adopt wholesale in their narratives.

Modern reinterpretations have, for many, transformed this intricate tapestry into a singular myth of omnipotent hidden power. In films, documentaries, and online forums, the Illuminati and Freemasons are often depicted as a monolithic entity controlling global events from the shadows. Iconic images such as the pyramid and the all-seeing eye on the U.S. dollar bill are cited as definitive proof of such influence. Nevertheless, in the rigorous analysis presented by academic sources—and as confirmed by archival evidence—the reality is considerably more fragmented and complex. Instead of a single cabal, a confluence of independent groups emerges, each reflecting a piece of the broader cultural and intellectual transformation initiated by the Enlightenment. Peer-reviewed articles, extensive archival studies, and detailed exegeses of ritual texts underscore that shared symbolism is a product of common cultural currents, not necessarily conspiratorial coordination.

In addition to historical documents and scholarly debates, modern cultural depictions have significantly amplified these myths. Popular media frequently condenses the exhaustive narratives of secret societies into appealing tropes of conspiracy and global domination.

Websites, sensationalist books, and blockbuster movies thrive on such simplified accounts, often citing details selectively from primary sources like Masonic ritual texts or surviving Illuminati correspondences. While these portrayals capture the imagination, they regularly lack the nuance that careful historical inquiry provides. The historical record, when examined holistically—from anti-Masonic literature of the 18th century to modern scholarly articles on secrecy and symbolism—reveals a far more intricate and diverse set of motivations, practices, and outcomes.

Digital archives and online repositories have only deepened public access to the myriad documents detailing secret society practices. With digital facsimiles of centuries-old manuscripts, detailed photographic records of ritual items, and interdisciplinary analyses available at the fingertips of modern researchers, the tools for deconstructing these complex legacies have never been more robust. For instance, digitized collections of Masonic archives and Illuminati documents provide tangible insights into the language, symbolism, and hierarchical structures that defined these groups. Scholars can now cross-reference these materials with contemporary interpretations found on academic platforms like SpringerLink or scholarly journals such as those published by the Oxford Academic Press. These digital resources have facilitated a new era of transparency in the historical study of secret societies, even as they underscore the gap between documented evidence and popular myth.

The enduring appeal of secret societies lies in their historical actions and the profound human desire for mystery—a desire to believe that hidden forces operate behind the veil of everyday life.

The aesthetics of secrecy, with their layered meaning and ambiguity, continue to resonate as a counterpoint to modern transparency and accountability. Despite being debunked by careful scholarship, modern conspiracy theories persist precisely because they offer a seductive narrative that simplifies global power's complexities into a single, easily understood truth. However, while compelling in its simplicity, this portrayal neglects the rich tapestry of cultural, political, and intellectual factors that shaped these organizations during the Enlightenment and beyond.

An important dimension of this interdisciplinary examination is the recognition that secret societies have played diverse roles in different societies. In America, for example, fraternal orders such as the Freemasons have influenced political and civic life to an extent that is well documented in scholarly research. Studies published in academic journals demonstrate that these organizations were integral to the social fabric of early America—providing a network of mutual support and contributing to the civic engagement that helped forge the nation. Similarly, comparative studies of European secret societies reveal that these networks were often deeply intertwined with the ideological struggles of their time, serving as incubators for revolutionary ideas even as they functioned separately.

Ultimately, synthesizing archival documents, scholarly debates, and modern reinterpretations offers a compelling portrait of an era when reason, secrecy, and symbolism converged to produce some of history's most intriguing organizations. The overlapping rituals, shared iconography, and occasional dual memberships between the Illuminati, Freemasonry, and other esoteric orders are not evidence of a single secret conspiracy but instead of a multifaceted, culturally rich phenomenon. Each group, while borrowing from a common well of mystical symbols, pursued its distinct objectives—whether it was fostering personal moral development or orchestrating a covert political revolution.

In conclusion, the comprehensive narrative of secret societies during the Enlightenment—and their enduring impact on modern culture—reveals a world where symbolism, ritual, and secrecy intertwine to shape the destiny of nations and the collective imagination. The historical record, enriched by primary sources, detailed scholarly analyses, and evolving cultural interpretations, confirms that while the surface similarities among these groups are striking, their underlying motivations and practices were as diverse as the communities that spawned them. This intricate and layered legacy remains a powerful reminder of the human quest for hidden knowledge, the complexity of societal transformation, and the perennial allure of mystery in a world ever hungry for secrets.

Chapter Five

Growth & Opposition (1776–1784) Expansion, famous members, rising suspicion.

The rise of the Illuminati between 1776 and 1784 was defined by ambition and secrecy, expansion and paranoia. Adam Weishaupt, the society's founder, envisioned a movement that would transcend monarchy and religious authority, shaping thought through careful ideological guidance. Nevertheless, as the Illuminati grew, its very secrecy bred enemies, fueling suspicion that ultimately led to its suppression. This growth was substantial; within a few years, the organization blossomed from a handful of founders to an estimated membership of 2,000 to 3,000 individuals across various European nations, transforming it from a local academic club into a far-reaching network. The tension between concealment and influence defined the organization's trajectory, ensuring its name remained one of the most enduring forces in historical discourse even after its dissolution.

Secrecy, for Weishaupt, was not merely a protective mechanism—it was the backbone of intellectual transformation. No movement seeking to challenge entrenched institutions could afford to operate openly, and the Illuminati's structure reflected this necessity. Members were not immediately inducted into the organization's core philosophies; instead, they were exposed to fragments of ideology over time, gradually acclimating to radical thought without being overwhelmed by its implications. This process mirrored Socratic learning principles, ensuring recruits believed they had arrived at new understandings independently rather than through direct persuasion. By ascending to higher ranks, they had already internalized Illuminati's ideals, reinforcing their loyalty and ensuring ideological cohesion.

Weishaupt saw secrecy as an instrument not only of security but of control. It created a carefully curated intellectual path, where members felt their journey was self-directed, even though their ideological progression was carefully shaped by leadership. The organization thrived on exclusivity; recruits were constantly reminded that they were part of something greater, something concealed from those deemed unworthy. It reinforced psychological dependency, ensuring that members remained engaged, driven by the desire to uncover deeper layers of knowledge. However, secrecy had another effect—while it protected the group from external threats, it also heightened internal divisions.

Adolf Freiherr Knigge, instrumental in expanding the Illuminati's reach, recognized that secrecy alone was insufficient. Weishaupt's vision of a tightly controlled intellectual elite was sustainable only within a small circle. To wield influence, the Illuminati needed numbers, and for numbers, it required an existing structure within which recruitment could flourish. Freemasonry provided the perfect conduit. Masonic lodges already valued discretion, making them ideal grounds for embedding Illuminati ideals. Through Knigge's extensive Masonic connections and recruiting prowess, the Illuminati rapidly expanded beyond Bavaria, drawing in influential figures from across the German states, including renowned intellectuals like Johann Wolfgang von Goethe and Johann Gottfried Herder, as well as powerful aristocrats such as Duke Ernst II of Saxe-Gotha-Altenburg. These prominent recruits lent significant prestige and extended the society's reach into literary, scientific, and governmental circles. Members gained entry into political and intellectual institutions, quietly shaping policy and discourse without attracting immediate suspicion. This strategy ensured that the Illuminati did not merely exist as a secret society—it became a force within existing power structures, allowing its influence to spread even as its visibility remained minimal.

Knigge's expansionist approach created tensions within the organization. Weishaupt, an idealist focused on moral perfection and forming an intellectual aristocracy through slow, careful indoctrination, feared that rapid growth could compromise secrecy, exposing the Illuminati to external threats before its influence was firmly established. He saw secrecy as a form of intellectual refinement, where only the most capable minds should ascend to positions of influence. Conversely, Knigge, a pragmatist keenly aware of the mechanics of power and influence, believed that the Illuminati's strength lay in numbers. Each recruit was another opportunity to embed their ideology into broader political and intellectual networks. This ideological rift shaped the organization's internal debates, forcing leadership to consider whether secrecy was a tool for control or an obstacle to expansion.

Beyond recruitment, secrecy played a pivotal role in shaping perception internally among Illuminati members and externally among its opponents. Within the organization, secrecy created exclusivity, fueling loyalty by reinforcing that knowledge was a privilege reserved for those deemed worthy. Members were conditioned to desire deeper access, ensuring continued engagement while preventing ideological deviation. Cognitive dissonance played a role in this process. Recruits had to reconcile contradictions between their previous beliefs and the organization's teachings, leading them to embrace new perspectives as part of an intellectual journey rather than as an imposed doctrine. This method ensured that secrecy did not merely protect the Illuminati—it actively shaped its members into ideological agents, embedding its philosophy within their identities.

However, secrecy had another unintended consequence—it bred paranoia. The Illuminati's concealment of its true purpose-led outsiders to assume its influence far exceeded reality. Governments, particularly Bavaria, viewed clandestine intellectual movements as threats, not necessarily because of what they had accomplished but because of the uncertainty surrounding their potential. The mounting suspicion was not solely the result of the Illuminati's secrecy; it was actively fanned by a coalition of powerful opponents, particularly the resurgent Jesuit order (recently reinstated in Bavaria after its dissolution), conservative Catholic clergy, and aristocratic factions who viewed any challenge to traditional authority as a direct threat to their power. These Counter-Enlightenment forces capitalized on public anxieties, portraying the Illuminati as a nefarious sect aiming to dismantle all social order. Karl Theodor, Elector of Bavaria, understood this dynamic well. Fear thrives in ambiguity, and Theodor's administration capitalized on uncertainty to justify aggressive suppression. It was not enough to outlaw the Illuminati—the government had to ensure the public believed the suppression was necessary and that failure to act would lead to widespread political instability. Theodor's crackdown in 1784 was as much psychological manipulation as legal action. By portraying the Illuminati as a revolutionary force working in secrecy to undermine the monarchy, he transformed them into an existential threat. While direct plans for violent overthrow remained elusive, confiscated documents, including private correspondence and internal instructions, revealed the Illuminati's anti-Jesuit stance, their promotion of rationalism over religious dogma, their calls for radical social reform, and their ambitious infiltration strategy, all of which were deeply unsettling to the conservative Bavarian establishment.

Theodor's suppression strategy was methodical. He framed the Illuminati not simply as political dissidents but as architects of social subversion, ensuring that their eradication was seen as a necessary act of governance. Public trials and forced confessions reinforced the narrative that Bavaria was actively defending itself against an unseen enemy. The crackdown was about dismantling the Illuminati and shaping how history would remember them. Theodor ensured that their real or imagined influence would persist in political discourse by portraying the group as a shadowy network working in secrecy to destabilize the monarchy. Even after suppression, their legend remained intact.

This government-induced paranoia did not merely end the Illuminati—it ensured its legend would persist. Suppression, rather than erasing the group, immortalized it. The Bavarian government's aggressive stance ensured their name carried weight even after the Illuminati's formal dissolution. The fear Theodor cultivated fed posthumous speculation, turning whispers of secret influence into a firm belief that the Illuminati had survived in hidden corners of governance. Reality mattered less than perception; secrecy did not die with the Illuminati—it was reborn in conspiracy.

Secrecy's paradox extended beyond government opposition. It ensured that the Illuminati's methods of control continued to function even after suppression. While many secret societies relied on overt rebellion, the Illuminati thrived on strategic infiltration, embedding members within institutions rather than challenging them directly. This distinction made suppression all the more difficult. Even as Bavarian officials sought to dismantle the organization, members already held positions within academia, bureaucracy, and religious councils, ensuring that their ideas continued to influence thought long after their formal membership had ended. Theodor's administration, attempting to destroy the Illuminati, had inadvertently

created an ideological framework that continued to exist without
needing the structure of a secret society.

Chapter Six

The Role of Espionage & Secret Communications —How secrecy played a crucial role.

Secrecy was not merely a protective measure for the Illuminati—it was the force that defined their existence and shaped their approach to influence, survival, and control. Where open defiance risked exposure and destruction, secrecy allowed them to operate unseen, embedding themselves within institutions and subtly shaping political and intellectual movements. Their mastery of concealment extended beyond simple discretion; a carefully engineered system of cryptographic communication, internal psychological conditioning, and the strategic deployment of misinformation and intelligence gathering made them not just an organization but an enduring force in the narrative of hidden power. While their primary operational secrecy focused on protecting their own, the Illuminati also engaged in a nascent form of espionage, discreetly collecting information on rivals and potential recruits and subtly propagating narratives favorable to their cause within influential circles, often blurring the lines between internal security and external manipulation.

The encoded language was central to their operations, ensuring that their messages could travel unseen by adversarial forces. Members relied on substitution ciphers that transformed letters into symbols or numerical values to maintain secrecy, rendering intercepted correspondence unreadable to outsiders. However, they understood that simple encryption was vulnerable to pattern detection and decryption techniques by state-sponsored cryptographers. To combat this, they introduced layers of polyalphabetic ciphers, shifting letter values according to predetermined keys that evolved at regular intervals. The foundation of their cryptographic ingenuity drew from existing encryption techniques while advancing their complexity to new levels. However, such intricate methods were often cumbersome and time-consuming, limiting the sheer volume of communications and requiring trusted couriers to physically transport the encoded messages at a vulnerable point in their network. Their methods bore striking similarities to early cryptographic pioneers such as Blaise de Vigenère, whose cipher introduced a revolutionary variable-shifting system based on a keyword. This method ensured that intercepted letters would be meaningless without the corresponding key. Like Vigenère, the Illuminati recognized that concealment was not simply about preventing interception but ensuring that even possessing sensitive material would be useless without knowledge of its underlying structure.

Surviving documents from the period reveal fascinating examples of Illuminati cryptographic techniques. Some letters were written in a mix of substitution codes and numerical encoding, wherein commonly used words were assigned abstract symbols, frustrating decryption attempts by government agents. More advanced techniques involved rotating cipher keys that changed with each exchange, preventing outside forces from establishing linguistic patterns. Layered encryption suggests a mastery of coded language and an awareness of counterintelligence efforts against them. They understood that secrecy was an asset and a battlefield, requiring constant adaptation and refinement to outmaneuver their pursuers. Their cryptographic expertise did not arise in isolation but was influenced by earlier encryption traditions practiced across European courts, religious institutions, and military factions. The ability to encode and obscure messages was not just a sign of intelligence but an assertion of control over information.

While their cryptographic methods allowed them to shield their internal communications, the broader development of encryption did not halt their dissolution. The secrecy they perfected became foundational to later intelligence organizations as cryptography advanced through the centuries. The emergence of mechanized encryption in the twentieth century—such as the Enigma machine used by Germany during World War II—built upon polyalphabetic principles first explored centuries earlier. The same core concept of encoding messages with evolving cipher keys remained integral to espionage networks across Europe and beyond. Even modern cybersecurity relies on encryption techniques with roots in these early methods, ensuring that digital communication remains protected from unwanted interception. Though the Illuminati may not have directly influenced these developments, their reliance on secrecy ensured that cryptographic advancement became an enduring necessity in intelligence operations.

Nevertheless, secrecy extended beyond technical encryption—a philosophy shaping the psychology of those within the organization. Members were conditioned to believe that hidden knowledge carried greater truth than publicly accessible information, reinforcing that Enlightenment was reserved for the initiated. Recruits were exposed to ideological teachings in stages, ensuring that deeper layers of thought felt earned rather than imposed. This sense of exclusivity intensified devotion, creating a psychological hierarchy where understanding of doctrine was not simply acquired but bestowed upon those deemed worthy. The process mirrored methods seen in religious orders, intelligence agencies, and cult-like structures, where secrecy became a mechanism for controlling individual commitment. This profound reliance on secrecy, while strategically rational for their goals, also raised ethical questions about transparency and manipulation, criticisms that would later be leveraged against them by their opponents who argued such methods were inherently undemocratic.

The conditioning reinforced a more profound truth: secrecy discouraged dissent. Those who questioned the hierarchy were excluded from advanced discussions and denied access to the privileged knowledge they once sought. The fear of ostracization functioned as an invisible enforcement system, where deviation did not bring immediate punishment but an implicit loss of status within the inner circle. It ensured that loyalty was self-reinforcing. The more members learned, the more they became unwilling to step away, lest they lose access to the concealed knowledge that defined their belonging.

Beyond psychological conditioning, secrecy functioned as a mechanism of isolation within the organization. The very nature of secrecy required that members limit their interactions outside the group to avoid exposure, creating an insular network where information circulated only within approved channels. This isolation reinforced dependence, ensuring members became deeply entrenched within the organization's inner workings. This structural insularity has been observed in later intelligence agencies and clandestine operations, where restricted access to information prevents fragmentation but fosters an environment where trust is constantly tested.

Isolation was not merely an external necessity—it shaped how members interacted within the group. The constant specter of infiltration bred an atmosphere of skepticism, where trust was measured by unwavering commitment rather than familiarity. It was common for members to operate in cells with limited direct knowledge of other operatives, a method later mirrored in espionage organizations that structured their networks to minimize exposure in case of infiltration. In many ways, secrecy became its paradox—the thing that protected the organization also created conditions for internal uncertainty. Moreover, for those members tasked with active infiltration into existing institutions, the constant pretense and potential for identity conflict added another layer of psychological burden, testing their unwavering loyalty.

As secrecy tightened its grip, it began affecting members in ways that extended beyond loyalty and internal structure. Some undoubtedly found a sense of purpose within the exclusivity of secret knowledge, yet others struggled with the psychological toll of existing within a permanently obscured reality. The constant need for discretion, coded messages, and the fear of exposure must have weighed heavily on those seeking something more tangible than ideological mysticism. This paranoia, inevitable in any group driven by secrecy, may have contributed to the fractures that ultimately led to exposure. An organization obsessed with protecting its knowledge had become vulnerable to the very suspicion it fostered. No encryption system, no matter how advanced, could protect against the unpredictability of human allegiance.

Secrecy carried inherent dangers. By operating in shadows, they became vulnerable to infiltration and betrayal from within. Disillusioned members who had grown weary of ideological exclusivity exposed key figures and decrypted correspondence, offering Bavarian authorities the intelligence they needed to dismantle the organization. The crackdown of 1784 was not merely a legal suppression but a psychological unraveling—secrecy, once their greatest weapon, had become their downfall. Without the shield of encoded communication, their internal networks collapsed, unraveling their influence within institutions.

Despite their dissolution, their legacy endured, transcending their physical existence and becoming an archetype of clandestine control. The secrecy that once protected them transformed into myth, ensuring that their reputation as masters of espionage never faded. The techniques they pioneered—covert infiltration, encoded communication, ideological secrecy, and misinformation—did not vanish but found new life in the structures of modern intelligence organizations. Their influence lingered not in direct continuity but in the continued association of secrecy with elite control. Whether they physically survived beyond their suppression mattered far less than the permanence of their tactics.

The paradox of secrecy is that its power is both survival and destruction. It shields influence but breeds paranoia, fortifies alliances but fosters isolation, protects ideas, and ensures that betrayal carries catastrophic consequences. The Illuminati's legacy is not defined by their material operations but by the philosophical weight of their secrecy itself. Their existence may have faded, but the idea of their unseen hand remains forever embedded in discussions of power, control, and intelligence.

Chapter Seven
Were They Truly a Threat? —Examining Bavaria's crackdown.

In the late 18th century, Bavaria stood at the threshold of intellectual transformation, caught between the powerful forces of Enlightenment philosophy and the deeply entrenched structures of monarchy and religious authority. The Illuminati, founded by Adam Weishaupt in 1776, emerged from this ideological tension, promoting reason and free thought and dismantling hierarchical constraints that had long dictated governance and belief. Their ideals aligned with a broader intellectual movement that questioned inherited power, the authority of the Catholic Church, and the limits placed on human inquiry. Unlike radical political movements that sought direct revolutionary change, the Illuminati focused on intellectual refinement, embedding their ideas into elite circles and covert networks rather than engaging in open defiance. However, their secrecy, infiltration of Masonic lodges, and hierarchical organization made them appear suspect to Bavarian rulers. It led to concerns that their ambitions extended beyond philosophy into calculated influence over government structures.

Elector Charles Theodore, tasked with maintaining stability in a politically cautious Bavaria, regarded these developments with increasing alarm. Reports suggesting that Illuminati influence had expanded among scholars, officials, and established institution members prompted suspicions that an unseen ideological force was operating beyond state oversight. While concrete proof of subversive activity was absent, perception alone was enough to justify action. The suppression of the Illuminati was swift and decisive, beginning with the formal ban on secret societies in 1784 and culminating in targeted arrests, the confiscation of documents, and the forced exile of Weishaupt. Bavaria presented the crackdown as a necessary defense against ideological subversion, reinforcing the belief that secret societies, regardless of their activities, posed a fundamental threat to political stability.

The psychology of suppression offers insight into why Bavaria acted with such force. Governments historically react most aggressively to movements that they cannot fully monitor or control. Secrecy breeds distrust, and in the absence of transparency, officials often fill gaps in knowledge with speculation, transforming ideological discourse into perceived conspiracy. The Illuminati embodied this dynamic—an intellectual circle operating discreetly within academic and political spaces, communicating through encrypted writings, and selectively recruiting members rather than engaging in open debate. Their presence within Freemasonry further complicated their position, as Masonic lodges had already been viewed with suspicion across Europe. While no direct revolutionary action had been proven, the assumption that their influence could be far-reaching was enough to trigger suppression.

This pattern is not unique to Bavaria. The historical tendency to dismantle ideological movements before they gain traction is well documented. Monarchies in France were wary of Enlightenment thinkers spreading critiques of inherited rule, imposed censorship, and restricted publications that questioned authority. Later, authoritarian regimes in the 20th century censored intellectual dissent before opposition could materialize, ensuring that philosophical movements could not develop into political challenges. The Illuminati followed this same trajectory—not dismantled for tangible political disruption but for the perceived potential of such disruption. Bavaria acted not on evidence of a conspiracy but on the fear that allowing unmonitored intellectual shifts to flourish could lead to societal instability.

Philosophically, the suppression of the Illuminati highlights the long-standing tension between progress and control. The Enlightenment championed rational inquiry, empirical reasoning, and dismantling structures that limited knowledge. However, Bavaria, heavily influenced by the Catholic Church, saw these principles as dangerous rather than transformative. The Illuminati's rejection of religious orthodoxy and their advocacy for secular reasoning placed them in direct conflict with clerical institutions that had long dictated the moral and intellectual framework of society. The Church, recognizing the threat posed by their philosophy, reinforced Bavaria's efforts to dissolve them, framing their elimination not only as a po-litical necessity but as a defense against ideological displacement.

Nevertheless, suppression does not always erase movements. The Bavarian crackdown ensured that the Illuminati did not disappear into obscurity but instead transitioned into legend. Instead of being remembered as an Enlightenment-era intellectual group, they be-came synonymous with secrecy, unseen influence, and global con-spiracy theories. Their dissolution created the illusion that they had gone underground, fueling speculation that they had continued to operate beyond the reach of Bavarian authority. Over the next two centuries, their name became less tied to their historical origins and more to broader narratives of clandestine power. The government's attempt to neutralize them unintentionally ensured their legacy would persist well beyond their years of activity.

Bavaria's legal framework further shaped the suppression. While the Illuminati was the most visible organization targeted, their dis-solution was not a standalone event—previous statutes had already established restrictions on underground ideological networks. Secret societies were framed as inherently destabilizing, allowing the gov-ernment to justify suppression as part of its ongoing efforts to regu-late intellectual movements. This precedent meant their elimination was not presented as a reactionary crackdown but as an extension of Bavaria's legal mechanisms for maintaining control over ideological forces beyond direct oversight.

Beyond immediate governmental actions, the effects of suppres-sion were felt throughout Bavaria's academic institutions. Universi-ties, long viewed as spaces for philosophical exploration, were subject to increased scrutiny. Professors and students aligned with Enlightenment ideals were pressured to conform their teachings to sanctioned doctrines, reinforcing an atmosphere of caution in intellectual circles. While suppression eliminated the Illuminati as an organization, it did not erase their ideas—philosophical discourse merely adapted, shifting into quieter, more discreet settings.

With the Illuminati officially dissolved, Bavaria had succeeded in eliminating a perceived ideological threat, but the consequences of their suppression extended far beyond their immediate dissolution. Government surveillance over intellectual gatherings intensified, and skepticism toward secret societies became a lasting feature of Bavarian policy. Other European states took note of Bavaria's success in neutralizing clandestine movements, reinforcing a broader crackdown on ideological organizations throughout the continent. The suppression of the Illuminati became a precedent for how governments could regulate underground intellectual societies, shaping how future organizations were monitored and dismantled.

The aftermath of suppression revealed an unintended consequence: instead of silencing their influence, Bavaria's actions ensured their transformation into a lasting historical phenomenon. Intellectual movements that faced government suppression often reappear in altered forms, and the Illuminati were no exception. Their philosophical ideals, once confined to Enlightenment-era Bavaria, were adapted and reinterpreted over time, influencing later ideological movements and providing inspiration for secret societies that followed. Initially tied to intellectual refinement, their name morphed into a symbol of global power structures operating in secrecy, a transformation shaped more by government fear than by their actions.

Despite all efforts to erase them, the Illuminati did not vanish from history. Their dissolution ensured that speculation about their continued existence flourished, evolving into mythologies and extending their influence beyond Bavaria. Governments frequently attempt to control narratives, but suppression often fuels the mystique surrounding banned organizations. By dismantling them, Bavaria did not erase the Illuminati—it ensured that their name would forever be tied to secrecy, conspiracy, and unseen influence.

Chapter Eight

Illuminati Influence on Revolutionary Movements –Their rumored role in political upheavals.

The Illuminati's alleged influence on revolutionary movements remains one of the most debated aspects of their legacy. Their dissolution in Bavaria in the mid-1780s officially marked the end of their formal existence, yet speculation about their intellectual footprint continued well beyond their immediate suppression. Questions persist regarding whether their members, expelled from Bavaria, carried their ideas into underground networks that contributed to political upheavals across Europe and the Americas. The French Revolution, in particular, is frequently cited as a historical moment where their ideological framework may have played a role. While direct evidence confirming their involvement remains elusive, the alignment of Illuminati philosophy with revolutionary rhetoric fuels the argument that their influence may have extended into the broader intellectual movements that shaped political revolutions. Furthermore, the very nature of their suppression by Bavarian authorities, characterized by public decrees and coerced confessions, inadvertently fueled the perception of the Illuminati as a potent, hidden threat, laying the groundwork for later conspiracy narratives.

The nature of their alleged impact on revolutionary movements is difficult to define because it exists at the intersection of confirmed ideological diffusion and more speculative claims about clandestine orchestration. This inherent ambiguity defines a central historiographical debate surrounding their legacy: Were they architects of revolution or simply a reflection of broader intellectual currents? What is certain is that former members of the Bavarian Illuminati did not simply vanish after suppression. Many continued their intellectual work, influencing reformist circles and Enlightenment-based political thought. The same core principles—opposing monarchical absolutism, advocating for secular governance, dismantling aristocratic privilege, and promoting rationalism—were fundamental to revolutionary discourse. The question is whether former Illuminati members actively participated in revolutionary activities or if their philosophical contributions were merely absorbed by broader movements without direct coordination.

The French Revolution represents one of the strongest cases of potential Illuminati influence. Enlightenment ideals formed the foundation of the revolution, providing the intellectual framework for those seeking to overthrow hereditary rule and replace it with a system guided by reason, equality, and individual liberty. The Illuminati's core ideological mission resembles the revolutionary objectives of 1789, particularly in their emphasis on rational governance and their rejection of religious authority dictating political power. While historical accounts do not explicitly document Bavarian Illuminati figures taking part in revolutionary planning, writings from the period indicate familiarity with their philosophy among revolutionary thinkers. Secret networks were undoubtedly active during the pre-revolutionary period, and some accounts argue that Illuminati-style organizational structures influenced the radicalization of individuals who became central figures in revolutionary activities, notably elements within the Jacobin clubs. The secrecy of these operations makes verification difficult, yet the similarities in ideological foundations remain striking. It is crucial to note that many of these early accusations emerged from reactionary circles seeking to delegitimize the revolutionary ideals by attributing them to a hidden, nefarious cabal rather than legitimate social and political grievances.

Beyond France, the American Revolution has also been linked, albeit loosely, to Illuminati influence. The independence movement, rooted in Enlightenment thought, bore philosophical similarities to the Illuminati's advocacy for rational governance, separation of power, and individual liberty. Some theorists propose that while no Bavarian Illuminati members were directly involved in American revolutionary activities, their ideals permeated through shared intellectual circles, particularly within Freemasonic lodges. Freemasonry, which played a prominent role in revolutionary discourse, carried many of the same rationalist and anti-monarchical sentiments that defined the Illuminati's mission. It leads to speculation that while the Illuminati may not have actively shaped the revolution, their intellectual influence may have found indirect pathways into revolutionary frameworks through overlapping ideological movements.

Looking beyond the 18th century, the revolutionary uprisings of the 19th century further raise the possibility that Illuminati philosophy persisted despite their official dissolution. The liberal nationalist movements that defined Europe's political landscape throughout the 1800s carried strong echoes of Illuminati ideals. The revolutions of 1848, often called the "Springtime of Nations," sought constitutional governance, democratic representation, and the removal of monarchical absolutism—goals deeply aligned with the Bavarian Illuminati's original vision. While there is no documented evidence confirming Illuminati involvement, the question remains whether ideological remnants survived within secret political societies that took shape in the decades following Bavaria's suppression of their organization. Revolutionary movements frequently draw from existing intellectual traditions, and it is plausible that Illuminati philosophies were absorbed into broader reformist networks without the need for direct organizational continuity.

The difficulty in analyzing the Illuminati's influence on revolutions lies in separating historical reality from myth. The idea that they orchestrated global upheavals from the shadows has been perpetuated by conspiracy theories that overstate their influence while ignoring broader intellectual and structural forces that shaped revolutionary movements. Key among these early narratives were the influential works of Abbé Augustin Barruel and John Robison, whose late 18th-century accusations of Illuminati and Masonic plotting against monarchies and the Church became foundational texts for subsequent conspiracy theories. These claims often rely on circumstantial similarities between revolutionary rhetoric and Illuminati ideology rather than concrete evidence of direct involvement. Scholars emphasize that while Illuminati philosophy may have found resonance in revolutionary discourse, attributing major political transformations exclusively to their influence oversimplifies history. "The Enlightenment" provided the foundation for revolutionary thought, and it is far more likely that revolutionary figures were influenced by various intellectual sources rather than a singular underground society.

Despite the lack of definitive proof, the theory that the Illuminati played a role in shaping revolutionary movements persists in historical inquiry and cultural imagination. Their reputation as an organization devoted to intellectual transformation makes them an attractive subject for speculation. Whether they actively participated in revolutions or their ideas merely coincided with larger ideological movements is an enduring debate reflecting the tension between historical evidence and speculative interpretation. The persistence of Illuminati-related conspiracies suggests that their name remains tied to the Enlightenment and moments of political upheaval, where secrecy and intellectual radicalism converge in historical narratives.

Expanding further, the psychological dimensions of their alleged revolutionary influence must be considered. Secrecy itself has a profound effect on perception. Movements that operate in clandestine spaces naturally invite speculation about their reach, whether real or imagined. The Illuminati's emphasis on encrypted communication, selective membership, and covert structuring created an environment where their influence could be exaggerated simply because of their methods. This phenomenon, well documented in political psychology, explains why organizations that cultivate secrecy are often perceived as more powerful than they truly are. Whether their actual influence extended to revolutionary movements or their perceived influence created exaggerated narratives remains an open question.

Philosophically, the debate surrounding their revolutionary influence highlights the complex relationship between ideological continuity and organizational survival. Ideas do not require formal institutions to endure—they spread through individuals, texts, and intellectual debates long after their original proponents are suppressed. While Bavaria succeeded in dismantling the Illuminati as an entity, it could not eradicate the ideas that had inspired their movement. If former members carried these principles into reformist and revolutionary circles, their philosophical influence would have persisted without requiring direct coordination. It demonstrates that ideological movements, once initiated, often transcend their original frameworks, influencing political discourse even in the absence of organizational continuity.

Therefore, the Illuminati's potential role in revolutionary movements must be understood not in direct orchestration but as a case study of how suppressed ideologies can reemerge in different forms. Whether their ideas found new homes in underground networks or were absorbed into broader Enlightenment currents, their intellectual presence remained a subject of speculation long after their formal dissolution. However unproven, the persistence of their legacy in revolutionary discourse speaks to the enduring nature of suppressed philosophies that continue shaping historical narratives even when their originators have faded into history.

Chapter Nine
The Suppression of the Illuminati (1784–1790) – The bans, trials, and downfall.

The suppression of the Illuminati between 1784 and 1790 stands as one of the most consequential crackdowns on secret societies in European history. What began as a relatively small intellectual movement rapidly became the focus of heightened scrutiny as Bavarian authorities sought to regulate ideological networks operating beyond state control. While the Illuminati presented themselves as a philosophical society devoted to rational inquiry and intellectual refinement, the secrecy surrounding their activities created suspicion among government officials and religious authorities alike. Elector Charles Theodore, confronted with concerns that clandestine organizations could be wielding influence over political structures, initiated a decisive campaign to dismantle the Illuminati, framing their suppression as an urgent measure to preserve the stability of Bavaria. However, the government's exaggerated portrayal of the group as politically dangerous contributed to lasting perceptions of their influence well beyond their actual scope.

The first formal act against secret societies came in 1784 with an edict that broadly banned organizations outside government oversight. While this decree did not explicitly name the Illuminati, it signaled Bavaria's growing unease with unmonitored intellectual movements. Long accustomed to secrecy, the Illuminati attempted to adjust by operating with even greater discretion. However, their reluctance to dissolve or openly comply with Bavarian regulations only reinforced suspicions. The belief that the Illuminati were not merely engaging in philosophical discussion but actively working toward political destabilization took hold, leading authorities to escalate their efforts to eradicate the organization.

By 1785, Bavaria issued a second edict explicitly targeting the Illuminati, declaring them illegal and authorizing measures to dismantle their network forcibly. This decision led to a systematic effort to disband Illuminati lodges, arrest suspected members, and seize documents that could serve as evidence of subversive activity. The Bavarian government conducted raids, intercepted encrypted correspondence, and subjected captured members to interrogations. While much of the confiscated material consisted of philosophical discourse rather than revolutionary planning, the presence of coded writings and hierarchical structuring further cemented the perception that the Illuminati posed a legitimate political threat.

Adam Weishaupt, the organization's founder, became the central target of suppression. Facing imminent arrest, he fled Bavaria in 1785, seeking refuge under the protection of Duke Ernst II in Gotha. His exile marked the symbolic collapse of the Illuminati's formal structure, yet it did not end their ideological presence. Weishaupt continued writing and defending the Illuminati's mission, maintaining that their philosophy was rooted in Enlightenment and reason rather than political conspiracy. His works ensured that the Illuminati remained a subject of debate long after their Bavarian dissolution. However, the government's characterization of the suppression as a necessary response to ideological subversion framed the Illuminati as a dangerous underground force rather than a misunderstood intellectual society.

The trials and investigations that followed reinforced Bavaria's efforts to dismantle the Illuminati completely. Confessions often coerced and provided details about recruitment methods, coded communications, and internal hierarchies. Some members renounced their affiliation, hoping to avoid further persecution, while others insisted that their group had been unfairly maligned. The Bavarian government distributed reports outlining the findings of their investigations, aiming to justify their actions by presenting the Illuminati as a destabilizing force. These official publications shaped how the Illuminati were perceived within Bavaria and across Europe, where conspiracy theories about their survival and influence began to take root.

The Catholic Church played a decisive role in reinforcing the suppression, framing the Illuminati's rejection of religious orthodoxy as a direct challenge to moral and theological stability. Clerical authorities denounced their teachings, linking them to dangerous heresies that threatened the foundations of Christian belief. Sermons, religious publications, and official Church decrees further solidified the justification for their eradication, ensuring that opposition to the Illuminati was not merely political but deeply entwined with religious authority. This convergence between Church and state strengthened the crackdown, transforming suppression into a movement to preserve faith and governance.

The mechanisms Bavaria used to enforce suppression extended beyond direct legal action. While the government relied on edicts and public decrees, it also policed ideological spaces beyond formal trials. Universities, literary circles, and even social gatherings became subject to surveillance, ensuring that remnants of Illuminati thought could not quietly persist under new names. Professors, particularly those suspected of Enlightenment leanings, were pressured to conform through direct interventions or subtle but effective reputational constraints that limited their career advancements. Even outside Bavaria, the suppression resonated with institutions that had loosely associated with Illuminati members, influencing the broader academic landscape.

The long-term effect on political discourse in Bavaria and beyond was profound. The Bavarian government's aggressive response did not merely eliminate the Illuminati; it shifted how dissent was managed in the decades following their suppression. Leaders of future ideological movements took greater precautions to avoid government intervention. The visibility of the Illuminati's suppression ensured that other intellectual circles operated with an increased awareness of risk, sometimes leading reformists to water down their rhetoric or disguise their political intentions within more widely accepted academic or religious frameworks. This suppression delayed some reformist movements by several decades, demonstrating how ideological crackdowns extend beyond the immediate elimination of an organization.

The psychological ramifications on former Illuminati members were deeply personal. The suppression did not merely dissolve the organization; it fragmented personal relationships and individual careers. Some former members faced exile, others struggled with reputational damage, and some sought to erase any association with the Illuminati out of fear of continued persecution. The psychological toll on individuals forced into ideological silence speaks to a broader trend in history where suppression leaves behind not only political consequences but deeply personal ones. This effect was powerful in Bavaria, where those once affiliated with the Illuminati found themselves socially and professionally alienated, leading some to recant their beliefs entirely. Others maintained their philosophical positions quietly, contributing to underground intellectual networks that preserved Enlightenment thought long after the formal destruction of the Illuminati.

The Bavarian suppression contributed to the rise of later clandestine movements that adopted elements of the Illuminati's organizational structure. The fear generated by the crackdown reinforced the necessity of discretion, encryption, and indirect influence. Groups operating in the 19th century, such as revolutionary cells in

France and nationalist movements in Italy, borrowed tactics associated with secret membership, coded communication, and hierarchical structuring. The Bavarian suppression inadvertently created a blueprint for underground organization, demonstrating how the lessons learned from ideological persecution are often repurposed rather than erased.

The legacy of their suppression extended far beyond Bavaria's borders. Their forced dissolution ensured their reputation persisted through conspiracy theories, reformist movements, and political discourse. By eradicating them, Bavaria unwittingly solidified its place in historical legend, ensuring that the Illuminati would forever be associated with secrecy, conspiracy, and unseen influence. Their suppression, rather than eliminating their intellectual presence, gave rise to a mythology that would continue to shape discussions surrounding secret societies for centuries.

Chapter Ten
The Disappearance & Survival Theories – Did they vanish or go underground?

F or centuries, debates have raged over the true fate of suppressed movements. Few disputes are as enduring as the question surrounding the Illuminati after its suppression by the Bavarian government between 1784 and 1790. Official records claim that the organization was ruthlessly dismantled, its members exiled, its documents seized, and its ideological presence terminated. Nevertheless, the very act of suppression may not have signified the final page of its history. Instead, some argue that the Illuminati receded into a realm of secret influence, subsuming itself within other networks or even metamorphosing into an entirely underground ideological current. This predicament invites us to consider the historical events and the psychological and philosophical implications that arise when states attempt to silence radical ideas. Indeed, the timing of the Illuminati's suppression coincided with the burgeoning revolutionary fervor in France, creating a potent narrative vacuum that was swiftly filled by polemicists eager to attribute the ensuing upheaval to a hidden, malevolent hand.

Historical accounts of the Illuminati's downfall paint a picture of a regime determined to reorder society by eliminating subversive thought. Edicts proclaimed salvation from chaos by purging dangerous influences, while state agents executed their mandate with swift precision. However, as with many episodes of repression, the official narrative coexists with traces of a more ambiguous reality. Here, the tangible records—letters, edicts, and private correspondences preserved in scattered archival repositories—offer crucial insights. Although many of these documents were lost or deliberately obscured by the authorities, the surviving pieces have allowed historians to glimpse the duality of the era: on one side lay the imperious declarations of total eradication, and on the other side, fragments of clandestine communication that hint at an unquiet persistence. Indeed, some early anti-Illuminati polemicists, paradoxically, fueled the very idea of their survival by claiming the order merely went deeper underground, adapting to evade detection. Such primary evidence, taken from state archives, personal diaries, and secret dispatches, forms the bedrock of a more nuanced interpretation. It suggests that while the visible form of the Illuminati may have been forced into hiding, its embers never truly died.

The lively debates among scholars exemplify the robustness of historical inquiry in this area. Contemporary historiography reveals that the official suppression of the Illuminati was not as unequivocal as state records might imply. After scrutinizing the surviving documents and comparing them with contemporary accounts from eyewitnesses and opposition writings, several academics have argued that the state's narrative was constructed as a measure of political expediency rather than an absolute assessment of reality. This scholarly discourse, which places the Illuminati's fate amidst contested interpretations of what constitutes 'eradication' versus 'transformation,' is an illuminating example of how historical narratives are subject to revision as new evidence or reinterpretations come to light. Debates persist on whether the archival omissions were a product of systematic destruction or the inevitable decay of secret materials and how biases in state-sponsored narratives skew our contemporary understanding of clandestine networks. Though officially suppressed, many former Bavarian Illuminati members continued their intellectual work, influencing reformist circles and Enlightenment-based political thought. Weishaupt himself, though in exile in Gotha, continued to write extensively, publishing works that defended the Illuminati's original aims and subtly propagated its ideals, even as the organization no longer formally existed. Other former members also pursued careers in academia, government, and journalism, ensuring that Enlightenment principles, infused with some Illuminati-esque radicalism, remained part of public discourse.

One compelling avenue of survival theory posits that many of the suppressed Illuminati members found refuge within the ranks of Freemasonry. Freemasonry, with its long-established network of lodges and secret rituals, represented both a continuation of Enlightenment ideals and a haven for covert dissidents. The integration into

Freemasonry is underscored by thematic similarities in symbolism and intellectual inquiry and by tangible evidence found in Masonic records—evidence that points to overlapping membership and shared philosophical pursuits. Contemporary scholars have noted that while the official histories of both organizations are shrouded in mystery, the presence of similar operative language and esoteric symbolism offers a persuasive case for the continuity of ideas. When part of a suppressed movement adopted the mantle of an established organization, the result was a transformation rather than a termination; the intellectual legacy continued under a new guise, protected by rituals that emphasized secrecy over public assertion.

Alternatively, some historians maintain that the Illuminati did not so much seek refuge in another institution as they did deliberately retreat into an underground ideological continuum. In this view, the abrupt intervention of the Bavarian authorities forced a metamorphosis in tactics. Like water under ice finding secret channels beneath the surface, the core principles of the Illuminati—its commitment to reason, liberty, and the emancipation of thought—found new outlets in clandestine gatherings, encrypted letters, and private academies that operated far from the public eye. The notion of an underground existence is supported by scattered references in obscure pamphlets and coded correspondence between like-minded European intellectuals. These documents, though indirect, point to a sustained albeit covert transmission of ideas, often facilitated through informal literary societies, philosophical salons, and academic networks that transcended national borders. The shifting form of these ideas, from formal organization to diffuse networks of rebellious thought, reflects a historical pattern observed in many revolutionary movements: when visible structures are forcibly dismantled, the underlying currents of dissent often persist in more ambiguous and resilient forms.

This pattern is not unique to the Illuminati. A comparative analysis with other suppressed movements—such as the Carbonari in Italy, whose revolutionary fervor was similarly curtailed by state intervention—reveals striking parallels. Like the Illuminati, the Carbonari were driven by the pursuit of intellectual and political reform. Although their overt organizations were crushed, the spirit of their movement survived in subsequent waves of dissent and contributed to the eventual unification and reformation of Italian society. This trope of a suppressed movement merely receding to fight another day is a recurring motif in the history of resistance, providing both a psychological solace for adherents and a compelling narrative for external observers. The comparison illustrates how state repression frequently leads to the reconstitution of radical ideas in altered forms. Both cases remind us that political power may silence individual voices and organizations in the short term. However, it rarely quashes the broader ideological trajectories that gave rise to those movements. Instead, the ideas that underpin such movements can adapt, migrate, and resurface, often with transformative consequences that reshape the political landscape over time.

The psychological impact of such suppression is profound, imbuing the narrative with an almost mythic dimension. Declaring an organization extinct often has the paradoxical effect of elevating its memory in the public imagination. A society that overtly denounces a set of ideas frequently finds that those ideas acquire a kind of sacred potency—an allure born of forbidden knowledge. Thus, the myth of the underground Illuminati has thrived partly because the more resolute the state's pronouncements of eradication, the stronger the aura of mystique that surrounds them becomes. This psychological magnetism, where the repressed becomes a symbol of ultimate resistance, reveals much about the human inclination to valorize what is hidden and forbidden. The collective memory transforms a chapter of political suppression into an enduring emblem of intellectual rebellion, contributing to a cultural legacy that persists beyond its historical moment. Modern scholars in conspiracy theory studies have extensively analyzed this phenomenon and examine the sociological and psychological mechanisms through which such narratives gain traction and endure, often serving as simplified explanations for complex societal changes.

At its core, the story of the Illuminati invites reflection on the inherent tension between state power and the unyielding persistence of human thought. When authorities initiate measures to stamp out dissent, they are not merely seeking to control ideas but also attempting to reshape history in their image. However, history demonstrates that control over the narrative is always partial. The flood of evidence provided by archival records and the ongoing debates among scholars suggest that the relationship between suppression and survival is far more complex than a simple binary of life and death. Instead, this relationship unfolds as a dynamic interplay where the disappearance of a formal structure gives rise to a metamorphosis of ideas. Revolutionary currents may wane in their original form, but the ideals that once animated them often persist, undergoing transformations that make them even more resilient.

The interplay between visible destruction and hidden persistence is also reflected in the broader cultural impact of the Illuminati myth. Modern discussions of conspiracy and secret power are steeped in the legacy of historical precedents. While the ongoing operation of an underground Illuminati remains debatable, its conceptual resonance has profoundly influenced academic and popular discourse. The tension between state control and freedom of thought, explored at length by contemporary cultural theorists, resonates with how modern political and social movements harness historical suppression narratives to challenge current power structures. Examining these historical patterns reminds us that the struggle for intellectual freedom is an ongoing process that transcends individual moments of political repression.

In contemplating the fate of the Illuminati, one is struck by the realization that archival evidence, though fragmentary, continues to challenge the neat resolutions offered by official histories. The sparse records of secret meetings intercepted letters, and personal memoirs of those who witnessed the crackdown provide a counterpoint to sanitized government pronouncements. They suggest that behind the visible rupture of a campaign against dissidence lay a covert persistence that would inspire subsequent generations of thinkers and revolutionaries. The interplay between recorded history and the gaps left by deliberate destruction serves as a reminder that the whole story is rarely captured in official documents alone but also in the quiet, often indiscernible echoes of thought that defy complete eradication.

By weaving together these strands—from archival scrutiny to comparative analyses of similarly suppressed movements and the robust debates among historians—a more textured understanding of the Illuminati's fate emerges. The narrative transcends the simplistic dichotomy of being either fully eradicated or entirely surviving in a neat, concealed network. Instead, it reflects the multifaceted nature of ideological evolution, where suppression is not synonymous with annihilation and where the persistence of ideas is as much a story of adaptation as resistance.

Ultimately, the saga of the Illuminati is not merely an academic inquiry into a lost society but a profound commentary on the resilience of human thought in the face of oppressive power. The state's efforts to extinguish a radical idea often engender new forms of intellectual rebellion, ensuring that what was meant to be wiped out transforms and endures. The story highlights the limits of control over ideas and underscores the perpetual evolution of dissent. Each fragment of archival evidence, every contested interpretation in scholarly debates, and the resonances drawn from the histories of analogous movements remind us that ideas, once set into motion, are exceedingly challenging to recapture entirely. The enduring allure of the clandestine and the reified myth of an underground resistance speak to the timeless struggle for freedom. This struggle remains as pertinent today as it was in the turbulent years of the Enlightenment.

In this light, the account of the Illuminati serves not only as an exploration of a historical phenomenon but also as an invitation to reflect on the broader dynamics between authority and the unquenchable spirit of inquiry. It reminds us that even when political power appears to have triumphed victoriously, the subtle undercurrents of rebellion persist unexpectedly, continually reshaping our cultural and intellectual landscapes.

Chapter Eleven

Illuminati Legends & Influence (1800s–1900s) –How their legacy evolved in secret societies.

The 19th century was a time of upheaval, where revolutions reshaped nations, ideologies clashed, and the world teetered between progress and uncertainty. Amid these seismic shifts, one name continued to surface—not in official records or documented movements, but in whispers, accusations, and fevered imaginations searching for unseen forces behind history's grand transformations. The Illuminati, long thought extinguished, refused to fade. Their influence—or at least the idea of their influence—had transcended their original existence. This enduring myth was profoundly amplified by the chaos of the French Revolution, which, in the late 18th and early 19th centuries, served as the primary canvas onto which accusations of Illuminati orchestration were painted, mainly through the influential writings of polemicists like Abbé Barruel and John Robison. No longer just a secret society, they had become something more enduring: a legend, an accusation, a symbol. Could they have truly vanished, or had they merely learned how to exist unseen?

As the world grappled with the liberal revolutions of 1830 and 1848, the rise of nationalism, and the complex interplay of industrialization and early socialist movements, the myth of the Illuminati adapted. Their name surfaced in debates, their supposed influence woven into narratives of conspiracy and control. The political instability of the 19th century made the legend more potent as ruling elites sought explanations for why long-established systems were crumbling. In America, the Illuminati became an instrument of caution, invoked by conservative preachers warning of moral and political subversion. In Europe, their supposed survival was analyzed with a blend of fear and fascination, their image entangled with the rise and fall of secret movements.

While earlier secret societies had wielded influence in tangible ways, the Illuminati's transformation into myth blurred the lines between historical fact and psychological phenomenon. Unlike their documented predecessors, their continued existence could neither be proven nor entirely dismissed. This uncertainty allowed them to take on new conceptual forms within philosophical and political discourse. Their name became shorthand for hidden influence, an enduring emblem of secrecy. Whether they had truly vanished or remained hidden, their legend shaped perceptions of power in ways far beyond their original ambitions.

Politics absorbed and repurposed the Illuminati myth, weaponizing secrecy as a rhetorical tool. Governments and conservative ideologues found the helpful idea: if revolutions and ideological shifts could be explained as the work of an invisible cabal, then suppression of dissent became justifiable. The myth thus transitioned from a speculative concern among Enlightenment thinkers to a potent popular narrative used to justify political repression and social control, often fueled by fear of cultural decay. Fear of secret manipulators undermining monarchies, infiltrating governments, or eroding the moral foundations of society allowed authorities to consolidate control, urging citizens to resist movements deemed too radical or subversive. The Illuminati was no longer just a supposed entity but a convenient explanation for historical transformation. The burgeoning print culture of the 19th century—with its explosion of popular newspapers, pamphlets, and novels—acted as a powerful engine for disseminating these theories, allowing them to reach a far wider audience than ever before and embedding them deeply into the popular imagination.

Religious opposition continued to reinforce fears surrounding secret societies. Although the Illuminati had been officially disbanded, Catholic leaders, particularly in Europe, warned that clandestine organizations still threatened Christian values. Anti-Masonic rhetoric frequently blurred with Illuminati accusations, fueling speculation that remnants of the society had merged with other groups to continue their influence. The idea of hidden manipulators working to undermine tradition resonated with those who feared the era's rapid social and political changes.

Secret societies thrived in the 19th century, shaping intellectual and ideological currents. Freemasonry, Rosicrucianism, and various other groups carried forward themes of secrecy, Enlightenment, and hidden knowledge—whether intentionally inspired by the Illuminati or merely aligned with similar ideals. The interconnected nature of real and imagined secret organizations fueled speculation that some iteration of the Illuminati had survived in disguise, continuing to operate under new identities and shifting allegiances. Beyond these, a more sinister evolution of the conspiracy theory emerged in the latter half of the century: the insidious linking of the Illuminati and other secret societies with antisemitic narratives, portraying Jewish financiers or 'elders' as the true, hidden orchestrators of global events, a trope that would tragically culminate in fabrications like The Protocols of the Elders of Zion and contribute to devastating consequences in the 20th century. This fusion tragically deepened the myth's toxicity.

The psychology of hidden influence played an undeniable role in sustaining the myth. Rationalist thought had taken hold in intellectual circles, challenging superstition and embracing empirical inquiry, yet paradoxically, belief in concealed power flourished alongside it. The human mind struggles with accepting chaos—patterns are sought, and unseen hands are assumed to pull strings behind every revolution and unexplained historical shift. The Illuminati embodied this search for order, serving as a placeholder for the incomprehensible. The intellectual elite debated whether secret knowledge shaped civilizations and whether governance was dictated not by public institutions but by hidden masters whose identities were veiled in secrecy. The idea was intoxicating: a world where power was not where it seemed, where real decisions were made in shadows.

Beyond political and philosophical discussions, secrecy became a psychological phenomenon, influencing how people interpreted historical events. The Illuminati legend persisted not simply because governments and intellectuals spoke of them but because the human mind resisted accepting that governments and revolutions were merely the result of human nature and evolving ideology. Instead, people envisioned deeper architectures beneath events. Who truly wielded power? Was history a construct carefully shaped by unseen forces? These questions perpetuated the Illuminati's influence, ensuring its presence in conversations long after its documented existence had ended.

The transition from historical fact to cultural myth gained momentum as literature and speculative thought absorbed the Illuminati into broader narratives of secrecy, control, and hidden knowledge. Gothic novels, early science fiction, and popular adventure stories began to feature shadowy organizations reminiscent of the Illuminati, cementing their image in the public consciousness as archetypes of unseen power and manipulation. Writers engaged with the idea as history and a philosophical construct—an inquiry into the mechanisms of influence itself. By the late 19th century, the Illuminati had transcended history and entered the realm of intellectual pursuit, evolving into something intangible yet undeniable. If unseen architects dictated history, then the legend could never truly die.

Their name became intertwined with other mysteries—coded messages, lost knowledge, symbolic warnings. Fictional portrayals merged with political rhetoric, reinforcing the belief that an unseen force shaped reality beyond the reach of ordinary people. Some claimed remnants of their teachings influenced modern movements in science, art, and governance. Others saw them as proof that history itself had never been entirely transparent.

This transformation was not limited to political discourse or intellectual speculation—it permeated everyday life. Symbols associated with secret influence became more widely recognized, their meaning shifting with time. Some saw them as evidence of hidden truths, while others dismissed them as mere embellishments of human imagination. The Illuminati had become more than a lost organization—it had become a reflection of humanity's enduring fascination with secrecy. Was it proof that hidden forces dictated history or merely a collective manifestation of fear and curiosity?

That fascination endured well into the 20th century. The world stood on the precipice of profound geopolitical transformations: global conflicts, ideological revolutions, and technological advancements that redefined power structures. The Illuminati, once a historical entity, had become a psychological and cultural force that no longer required evidence to exist. It thrived in speculation, cautionary tales, and the continuous search for answers in history patterns. Whether invoked as a warning, feared as manipulation, or embraced as mystery, its legacy remained intact.

It had achieved something beyond mere survival; it had transcended history itself, living on as an idea—a belief that somewhere, behind the visible structures of power, a hidden hand still worked in silence.

Chapter Twelve
The 20th Century Revival of Illuminati Conspiracies – From Cold War fears to modern myths.

The Cold War was more than a geopolitical struggle—a battle of perception, secrecy, and fear. As nations raced to outmaneuver each other in intelligence operations, nuclear brinkmanship, and ideological warfare, the world became a stage for unseen forces. In this climate of uncertainty, conspiracy theories flourished, and among them, the legend of the Illuminati found new life. No longer just a relic of the 18th century, the Illuminati became a symbol of hidden control, whispered about in political circles, referenced in literature, and feared by those who saw patterns in the chaos of global events.

A convergence of political paranoia, religious millenarianism, and the rapid expansion of mass media shaped the 20th-century revival of Illuminati conspiracies. The Cold War era, heightened secrecy, espionage, and ideological battles provided fertile ground for theories suggesting that unseen forces orchestrated global events. Intelligence agencies such as the CIA and KGB engaged in psychological warfare, manipulating public perception through misinformation campaigns. While no direct evidence links the Illuminati to these efforts, the myth of a secret elite controlling world affairs became deeply embedded in narratives of espionage and global manipulation. The fear of unseen hands guiding world events became a potent force in shaping public opinion, reinforcing the idea that geopolitical shifts were not merely the result of competing ideologies but of deliberate orchestration.

Religious millenarianism played a significant role in the resurgence of Illuminati conspiracies. Evangelical movements and apocalyptic theorists framed the Illuminati as agents of the Antichrist, blending political paranoia with eschatological concerns. The notion of a New World Order gained traction, with some believing that a secret cabal sought global domination, the erosion of national sovereignty, and the subversion of religious institutions. This fusion of political and theological fears created a compelling narrative, particularly among groups that perceived rapid societal changes as evidence of a concealed agenda.

As the Illuminati myth evolved, it transitioned from a predominantly political conspiracy into a broader cultural symbol. The proliferation of mass media, particularly television and film, allowed Illuminati imagery to permeate entertainment. Symbols such as the All-Seeing Eye, pyramidal structures, and cryptic motifs became recurring elements in visual storytelling, reinforcing the idea that secret

societies actively shaped contemporary society. It was not inciden-
tal—filmmakers, authors, and musicians deliberately employed these
symbols to evoke intrigue, further embedding the Illuminati myth in
the collective imagination.

The impact of mass media on conspiracy proliferation cannot
be overstated. Sensationalized reporting, speculative documentaries,
and dramatic retellings blurred the boundary between historical reality and myth, making it increasingly difficult for audiences to dis-
tinguish fact from fiction. The rise of the internet accelerated this
phenomenon, providing a platform for independent researchers, discussion forums, and amateur theorists to construct elaborate narratives linking world leaders, financial institutions, and entertainment
figures to the Illuminati. The ability to connect seemingly disparate
events created the illusion of coherence, making even tenuous claims
appear credible.

The influence of early 20th-century secret societies added another
layer to the Illuminati myth. While the Bavarian Illuminati had long
been disbanded, other exclusive organizations—such as Skull and
Bones and the Bohemian Club—were sometimes linked to Illuminati conspiracies. Their secrecy, elite membership, and influence in
political and financial circles fueled speculation that secret groups
still operated behind the scenes. The idea that influential individuals
gathered privately to discuss global affairs reinforced the belief that
the Illuminati had not disappeared but had merely evolved into new
forms.

Economic instability also played a crucial role in the resurgence of
Illuminati conspiracies. Major financial crises, such as the Great De-

pression and the stagflation of the 1970s, reinforced fears that global elites were manipulating economies for their benefit. The Illuminati became a convenient explanation for economic downturns, particularly among those distrusting banking institutions and multinational corporations. The rise of international financial organizations, such as the International Monetary Fund and the World Bank, further fueled suspicions that a hidden network controlled global wealth and economic policies.

The psychological impact of secrecy and exclusivity contributed to the persistence of Illuminati conspiracies. The belief in secret societies is often fueled by the human tendency to seek hidden explanations for complex events. The idea that a small, elite group controls world affairs provides a sense of order in an otherwise chaotic geopolitical landscape. This psychological need for certainty and structure played a significant role in the 20th-century revival of Illuminati conspiracies, particularly during economic instability and political upheaval.

The role of intelligence agencies in shaping public perception cannot be ignored. While the Illuminati itself was not directly involved in Cold War espionage, the era's obsession with secrecy and covert operations reinforced the idea that unseen forces were manipulating global events. Governments engaged in misinformation campaigns, and intelligence agencies operated in the shadows, creating an environment where conspiracy theories thrived. The Illuminati became a convenient symbol for these fears, representing the unknown and the uncontrollable.

The rise of alternative media and underground publications in the late 20th century also contributed to the spread of Illuminati conspiracies. As mainstream media was increasingly viewed skeptically, independent researchers and fringe publications gained influence. Books, pamphlets, and later online forums provided a platform for theories that might have otherwise remained obscure. The Illuminati myth adapted to this new media landscape, evolving into a flexible narrative that could be applied to nearly any major event or political shift.

Public trust in institutions declined significantly in the latter half of the 20th century. Scandals such as Watergate, covert military operations, and financial crises fueled skepticism, reinforcing the belief that powerful elites operated in secrecy. The Illuminati became an expedient explanation for those seeking order in chaos—rather than accepting systemic failures, corruption, or geopolitical competition as natural occurrences, and many came to believe that a hidden group manipulated world events. The notion of an omnipresent secret society exerting control provided structure to an increasingly unstable world.

Despite the widespread belief in Illuminati conspiracies, historical evidence remains elusive. The original Bavarian Illuminati were dismantled in the late 18th century, and no verifiable proof exists that they continued in any organized form. The myth's persistence speaks more to society's psychological and philosophical needs than any tangible reality. In many ways, the Illuminati has become a metaphor for power itself—an embodiment of the fear that control is concentrated beyond the reach of ordinary individuals.

The 20th-century resurgence of Illuminati conspiracies was not merely a reflection of paranoia but a testament to the enduring allure of secrecy. Whether regarded as a genuine belief or a cultural phenomenon, the idea of a hidden elite guiding world affairs remains deeply embedded in public consciousness. The Illuminati myth will evolve as history progresses, adapting to new fears, emerging technologies, and shifting uncertainties, ensuring its relevance for future generations.

Chapter Thirteen

The Illuminati & Occult Symbolism —How symbols like the "All-Seeing Eye" became associated with secret power.

The all-seeing eye has long been a symbol of hidden power, appearing in religious iconography, secret societies, and conspiracy theories. While today many associate it with the Illuminati, its origins stretch far beyond the modern era, rooted in mysticism, philosophy, and humanity's enduring fascination with omniscience. The Bavarian Illuminati, founded in 1776, was primarily a rationalist organization focused on Enlightenment ideals, with little documented direct engagement in mystical or occult practices. However, as the fascination with secret societies grew—and particularly as Freemasonry and other esoteric traditions utilized rich symbolism—the mythology surrounding the Illuminati increasingly linked them to symbols that conveyed hidden knowledge and unseen influence, blurring histori-cal reality with later speculation.

Originally a representation of divine providence, the all-seeing eye was repurposed as a mark of surveillance, control, and Enlighten-ment. Throughout history, symbols have carried layers of mean-ing, evolving with cultural shifts and ideological movements. The all-seeing eye first appeared in religious contexts, often signifying divine omniscience. In Christianity, it was depicted within a triangle, representing the Holy Trinity. In ancient Egypt, the eye of Horus symbolized protection and wisdom. In ancient Mesopotamian and Hindu traditions, the eye was seen as a force of cosmic balance, ensuring justice and order. These interpretations laid the foundation for later associations with secret societies, where the eye became a metaphor for hidden knowledge and elite oversight.

The Illuminati's mythological connection to occult symbolism intensified in the nineteenth and twentieth centuries as conspiracy theories flourished. The inherent secrecy surrounding elite organiza-tions fueled speculation that they wielded esoteric power, using sym-bols to communicate their hidden influence. The all-seeing eye be-came a shorthand for surveillance and control, appearing frequently in literature and political discourse to evoke such hidden machina-tions.

Sacred geometry plays a significant role in much of the speculated Illuminati symbolism. The all-seeing eye is often enclosed within a triangle, a shape deeply connected to ancient mathematical and philosophical traditions. The triangle has been associated with balance, power, and hidden knowledge, reinforcing the idea that the Illuminati wielded esoteric wisdom. This geometric symbolism appears in architecture, religious iconography, and secret society emblems, further embedding the idea that specific shapes hold mystical significance.

The Pyramid: Foundation of Mystery

Beyond the all-seeing eye, the pyramid is another potent symbol deeply embedded in the Illuminati myth. The pyramid, an ancient architectural marvel, has long symbolized stability, hierarchy, and eternity across various cultures. In ancient Egypt, pyramids served as tombs and monuments, representing the ascent to higher planes and connections to divine power. This association with ancient wisdom and enduring structures made it a natural fit for esoteric traditions.

Within Freemasonry, the uncompleted pyramid (often called the 'capstone' or 'missing stone') can symbolize an unfinished work, the aspiration for perfection, or the ongoing construction of a moral and enlightened society. When the Bavarian Illuminati's alleged Masonic connections gained traction, the pyramid, already a staple of Masonic symbolism, was swiftly adopted into the burgeoning conspiracy narratives. The most famous instance, of course, is its presence on the reverse of the US dollar bill, topped by the all-seeing eye and the Latin motto 'Annuit Coeptis' (He approves our undertakings) and 'Novus Ordo Seclorum' (New Order of the Ages). This particular imagery, despite its official government interpretation, became a cornerstone of the Illuminati conspiracy, seen by theorists as undeniable proof of the society's continued, hidden influence in shaping world events and establishing a 'New World Order.'

The connection between the eye and ancient mysticism adds another layer to its enduring appeal. The eye of Horus in Egyptian mythology and the third eye in Hindu and Buddhist traditions symbolize heightened perception and Enlightenment. These ancient interpretations, alongside the influence of Hermeticism and alchemy, frequently referenced the eye as a symbol of transformation and hidden knowledge and contributed to the modern association of the all-seeing eye with secret knowledge and unseen control. The idea that specific individuals or groups possess hidden wisdom has fueled speculation about secret societies using symbols to mark their influence.

The all-seeing eye is also linked to initiation rituals and symbolic practices within secret societies. While historical evidence does not definitively link the original Bavarian Illuminati to the direct use of the all-seeing eye in their documented rituals, later conspiracy theories readily appropriated the symbol, suggesting it was used to mark those with access to secret knowledge. The idea that initiates were granted deeper understanding through symbolic rites has persisted in esoteric traditions. Occult literature and esoteric writings have further solidified the all-seeing eye's reputation as a mark of secret influence. Books on mysticism, alchemy, and secret societies often reference the eye as a gateway to hidden truths. The symbol's presence in these texts has reinforced its association with elite knowledge, making it a recurring motif in discussions about secret power.

Beyond secret societies, the all-seeing eye has appeared in corporate branding and institutional logos, fueling theories that influential organizations use occult symbolism to signal hidden control. These interpretations, often amplified by Illuminati conspiracy narratives, seize upon instances where companies and government agencies have incorporated triangular and eye imagery into their insignia, leading to speculation that these symbols are intentional markers of influence. While many of these designs are purely aesthetic or draw from independent traditions, their resemblance to esoteric symbols has contributed to the belief that secret groups operate behind the scenes.

The role of light and illumination in symbolism further reinforces the all-seeing eye's significance. The eye is often depicted surrounded by rays of light, reinforcing themes of Enlightenment and hidden knowledge. This imagery aligns with the Illuminati's name, which derives from the Latin Illuminatus, meaning enlightened. Using light as a metaphor for revelation reinforces the idea that secret societies possess hidden wisdom.

The all-seeing eye has even been incorporated into secret society architecture. Some buildings associated with secret organizations feature eye imagery in their design, reinforcing theories that these structures serve as markers of hidden influence. Whether in Masonic lodges, government buildings, or financial institutions, the presence of the all-seeing eye in architecture has led to speculation that these structures signal elite control.

The symbol has also been used in psychological manipulation. The all-seeing eye has been employed in propaganda and psychological operations to evoke feelings of surveillance and control. Governments and intelligence agencies have used similar imagery to reinforce authority, further embedding the idea that unseen forces monitor society. The all-seeing eye has also been linked to the broader notion of symbolic recognition among elite groups. Some believe the symbol was used as a discreet identifier among members of secret societies, allowing them to recognize one another without explicit acknowledgment. This theory aligns with historical accounts of secret handshakes, coded language, and symbolic gestures used by various clandestine organizations. Another aspect worth exploring is the psychological effect of surveillance imagery. Studies suggest that people modify their behavior when they believe they are being watched, even if the observation is symbolic rather than literal. The all-seeing eye taps into this instinct, reinforcing authority and compliance through its mere presence. This phenomenon has been leveraged in propaganda, corporate branding, and architectural design to influence human behavior subtly.

The symbol's presence in Renaissance and Enlightenment-era art further solidifies its connection to hidden knowledge. Paintings, sculptures, and architectural motifs often incorporated the all-seeing eye to represent divine wisdom, reinforcing its later association with secret societies. The idea that specific individuals or groups possess privileged knowledge has persisted throughout history, shaping how the symbol is perceived today.

The all-seeing eye has taken on new meanings related to artificial intelligence and surveillance in the modern era. The rise of facial recognition, predictive algorithms, and mass data collection has given the symbol a contemporary relevance, linking it to concerns about privacy and control. The idea that unseen forces monitor individuals has become a central theme in discussions about digital privacy, reinforcing the all-seeing eye's association with control. As governments and corporations expand digital surveillance, the all-seeing eye remains a powerful metaphor for modern concerns about privacy and oversight. While its historical roots are deeply tied to mysticism and divine observation, today, it represents a different kind of omniscience driven by technology rather than esoteric wisdom.

Chapter Fourteen

Influence on Literature & Fiction – From Angels & Demons to early works shaping perceptions.

The allure of hidden power and the promise of secret knowledge have long captivated human imagination, inspiring narratives that traverse history, philosophy, psychology, literature, and cinema. Across diverse cultures and epochs, secret societies have served as mirrors reflecting our deepest aspirations and as molds shaping collective consciousness. This chapter weaves ancient iconography, scholarly debates, and cinematic storytelling to explore how symbols—such as the all-seeing eye—evolved from emblems of divine protection into potent instruments of enforced truth.

In early civilizations, symbols like the all-seeing eye were imbued with profound spiritual significance. In ancient Egypt, the Eye of Horus was revered as a protective talisman, a manifestation of divine vigilance safeguarded against the unknown's chaos. Early Christian art adopted the all-seeing eye to represent an omnipresent deity over-seeing human morality. At the same time, various Eastern traditions utilized similar imagery to evoke spiritual awakening and the cultivation of inner wisdom. Over the centuries, however, the same iconography transformed. In modern popular culture—particularly within narratives involving alleged Illuminati machinations—the all-seeing eye is recontextualized as a symbol of clandestine, coercive power. This shift in symbolism, discussed extensively by scholars such as Nicholas Goodrick-Clarke and Richard Cavendish, reflects a broad-er debate: whether the act of illumination, meant to reveal hidden truths, might also impose a dogmatic uniformity, stifling individual freedom. Indeed, this tension was arguably present even within the historical Bavarian Illuminati's hierarchical structure, where knowl-edge was revealed in stages, and a controlled "Enlightenment" was offered to initiates, raising questions about whether their pursuit of reason inadvertently risked a subtle form of intellectual condition-ing.

The modern reimagining of these themes is strikingly evident in Dan Brown's Angels and Demons. In his narrative, the Illuminati are portrayed not as relics of history but as active agents whose secret orders manipulate symbols and rituals to shape public conscious-ness. Brown employs a rich array of imagery—from ambigrams and arcane sigils to the omnipresent all-seeing eye—to pose a provocative question: Can the concentration of knowledge within an elite cadre simultaneously liberate and oppress? His narrative challenges read-ers to consider whether the pursuit of truth risks distilling the rich plurality of human experience into a single, enforced vision when mediated by shadowy orders. The tension between Enlightenment and indoctrination in Angels and Demons echoes long-standing philosophical and psychological debates that have animated intellectual discourse since the Enlightenment when secret societies first emerged as both beacons of intellectual ambition and symbols of hidden tyranny.

An equally compelling narrative unfolds within the science-fiction realm of the Stargate illumination plot. Set several million years ago in the Alteran Home Galaxy, a council of advanced beings—the Ancients—grappled with the existential threat posed by an increasingly oppressive force known as the Ori. At the center of their debate was a visionary named Amelius, who proposed using a formidable device called the Ark of Truth. Designed to emit an overpowering beam of light capable of compelling its witnesses to accept a singular, immutable truth, the Ark promised a swift resolution to the growing menace of the Ori. Nevertheless, this prospect raised profound ethical and philosophical concerns among the Ancients. Fearing that such an act of forced illumination risked eradicating free will—the very spark of creative thought—they ultimately chose to abandon their home galaxy in search of a future where diversity of thought could flourish. This ancient dilemma is vividly resurrected when SG-1, the intrepid exploratory team from Earth's Stargate program, unearths a sealed relic amid the ruins of Dakara. Far from a mere weapon of destruction, the artifact bears the unmistakable legacy of the lost Ark, symbolizing an age-old struggle between the potential liberatory power of revelation and the inherent dangers of indoctrination.

When SG-1 activates the relic during an intense confrontation with Ori forces under the command of the determined Tomin, the device unleashes a dazzling beam of light. Rather than causing immediate physical devastation, this illumination functions as a symbolic act—a dramatic representation of imposed clarity that prompts both the characters and the audience to question whether enforced truth can diminish individual thought. The radiant emission simultaneously dispels the surrounding darkness while casting long, ambiguous shadows, evoking modern anxieties about digital surveillance and algorithmic governance. In an era where technological tools increasingly mediate our access to information and where individuals can become ensnared in ideologically reinforced "filter bubbles" or "echo chambers" that present a curated, often singular, view of reality, the narrative warns of the peril when truth is rendered an unyielding, monolithic force.

Cinematic narratives enrich this discourse by offering visual allegories that mirror the tension between revelation and repression. In Stanley Kubrick's Eyes Wide Shut, viewers are plunged into a labyrinth of masked rituals and clandestine gatherings, where an elite order operates beneath the comforting veneer of societal normalcy. The film's interplay of light and shadow—the imagery of closed doors, shifting silhouettes, and occult symbols—serves as a potent reminder that beneath even the most polished surfaces, hidden powers may exert subtle control over public and private lives. Kubrick's visual language blurs the boundaries between what is openly manifested and what remains shrouded in secrecy, compelling audiences to confront the uncomfortable possibility that the forces shaping their reality are as inscrutable as they are omnipresent.

Similarly, The Da Vinci Code translates historical intrigue into a modern quest for concealed truth, suggesting that venerable institutions may have long manipulated sacred texts and relics to maintain their stranglehold on authority. By reconfiguring secret societies as guardians of forbidden knowledge, the narrative invites viewers to interrogate the reliability of accepted historical records and to consider whether true Enlightenment is ever attainable when clandestine agendas so carefully partition information. The film contributes to a broader cultural narrative in which forced illumination—where truth is not discovered through inquiry but instead imposed—becomes a metaphor for both the promise and the peril of absolute power.

Films such as The Manchurian Candidate and The Ninth Gate introduce additional layers of complexity. In The Manchurian Candidate, the mechanisms of brainwashing and political subterfuge are exposed with chilling precision, revealing a world where a carefully orchestrated conspiracy overrides individual autonomy. This narrative underscores a timeless fear that imprinting a single "truth" on a collective can eradicate the vibrant spectrum of human thought. On the other hand, The Ninth Gate leads its characters into a cryptic realm populated by occult manuscripts and forbidden lore, where the obsessive pursuit of secret knowledge becomes both a pathway to transcendence and a precursor to self-destruction. These films resonate with a deep-seated skepticism regarding narratives in which truth is dictated rather than unearthed, echoing contemporary concerns over the gradual erosion of personal freedom through pervasive digital and algorithmic control.

Beyond the direct allegories, some works dive headfirst into the fabric of conspiracy. A seminal example is The Illuminatus! Trilogy by American writers Robert Shea and Robert Anton Wilson, first published in 1975. This satirical, postmodern, and science fiction-influenced adventure thrusts readers into a drug-, sex-, and magic-laden trek through a dizzying array of historical and imaginary conspiracy theories, all revolving around the author's version of the Illuminati. Rather than simply using the Illuminati as a shadowy threat, the trilogy directly engages with and deconstructs the nature of belief, reality, and hidden power, making it a pivotal text in the evolution of modern conspiracy culture. It embodies the ultimate "forced illumination" by overwhelming the reader with conflicting truths, leaving them to question the possibility of objective reality.

Even within superhero and gothic narratives, the tensions between personal autonomy and enforced doctrine are unmistakable. In Batman Begins the League of Shadows is portrayed as an enigmatic organization whose ancient traditions and rigid ideologies exemplify the eternal conflict between individual freedom and the homogenizing effects of collective power. The film subtly suggests that imposition a singular vision, even in the name of justice, can risk reducing the nuanced human experience to a set of dogmatic imperatives. Tim Burton's Sleepy Hollow further explores these themes through its gothic reimagining of ancestral secrets and occult forces, reinforcing the notion that the mysteries encoded in our past continue to cast long, influential shadows over the present.

In bringing all these diverse narratives together, a persistent philosophical tension emerges: Can the act of illumination, whether in ancient rituals, literary thrillers, or modern cinematic representations, truly liberate society, or does it invariably impose a constrictive uniformity? As explored by historical scholars and contemporary philosophers, the answer is far from straightforward. On one hand, Enlightenment offers the promise of clarity and dispelling ignorance. Conversely, when knowledge is rendered an absolute, unchallengeable mandate, it risks quashing the diverse perspectives underpinning a healthy, dynamic society.

The all-seeing eye, with its multiple layers of meaning, encapsulates this duality. Once a symbol of divine guardianship and spiritual awakening, it has been repurposed in modern narratives to denote both protective oversight and authoritarian control. This evolution—the subject of much debate in scholarly circles—reflects broader cultural fears that the mechanisms designed to reveal truth might ultimately become instruments for its imposition. In our current digital age, where surveillance technology and algorithmic decision-making increasingly influence our daily lives, these warnings are more resonant than ever.

Moreover, the psychological ramifications of forced illumination are profound. Human cognition is wired to thrive on a delicate balance between the desire for certainty and the need for critical inquiry. While there is an inherent human attraction to clear, definitive answers in a complex world, when truth is delivered in a singular, unyielding form, it risks eclipsing the richness of individual thought. It creates a dependency on external arbiters of knowledge.

This outcome undermines the organic, ever-evolving nature of understanding. This ambivalence lies at the heart of debates over modern technology's role in shaping our perceptions and lives, echoing the core concerns expressed in literary and cinematic explorations of secret societies.

By seamlessly integrating these diverse discussions—from the reimagined Illuminati of Angels and Demons to the cosmic deliberations over the Ark of Truth in the Stargate narrative, from the visual allegories of Eyes Wide Shut and The Da Vinci Code to the political and psychological inquiries of The Manchurian Candidate, The Ninth Gate, and the meta-narrative of The Illuminatus! Trilogy—we arrive at a comprehensive examination of forced illumination as both a liberatory and a coercive force. These interconnected narratives compel us to ask whether the quest for absolute clarity can coexist with the sustenance of individual autonomy or whether the imposition of a singular vision will inevitably curtail the complexity inherent in human experience.

Ultimately, the legacy of secret societies and their symbolic paraphernalia reveals a multidimensional struggle for dispelling ignorance and preserving the pluralism essential to a vibrant, progressive society. As we continue to navigate an increasingly interconnected world, where digital networks and surveillance systems loom large, the lessons encoded in these narratives are both a beacon and a warning. They remind us that every act of illumination carries the dual potential for liberation and constraint. Embracing this complexity, we are encouraged to remain ever-vigilant in our pursuit of knowledge, to challenge the sources of authority, and to celebrate the diversity of perspectives that enrich our shared human experience.

Chapter Fifteen

Modern-Day "Illuminati" & Pop Culture –How they're portrayed in media.

In contemporary culture, the myth of the Illuminati has transformed from a narrowly defined historical phenomenon into a dynamic cultural archetype that pervades modern media and popular discourse. This reimagined symbol is no longer confined to clandestine societies of the 18th century or the treatises of Enlightenment thought; instead, it leverages those historical roots, transformed into a potent emblem of power, control, and hidden truth amid the complexities of a rapidly evolving global landscape. The myth enthralls partly because it taps into deep-seated psychological impulses—most notably, the human tendency toward patternicity—and partly because it serves as a canvas upon which modern anxieties about surveillance, technology, and institutional dominance are vividly painted.

The cinematic portrayals of the Illuminati have been especially influential in shaping our contemporary perceptions. Films have reconfigured the secret society into an omnipresent force that can shape historical narratives and control overarching social currents. In such works, symbols like the all-seeing eye appear repeatedly—not merely as decorative motifs but as loaded symbols that evoke divine oversight and the potential tyranny of authoritarian control. The interplay of shadow and light on the screen creates a visual tension that mirrors the conceptual duality of the myth. Here, the seductive allure of hidden knowledge is counterbalanced by the fear that such knowledge, when monopolized by an unseen elite, may suffice to quash individual autonomy. Through these cinematic narratives, viewers are invited to question whether the promise of absolute truth is worth the risk of surrendering the plurality of human experience to a single, monolithic authority.

Unlike film, popular music also deploys Illuminati symbolism as a cultural critique. Many artists, especially in genres such as hip-hop and pop, have incorporated imagery associated with secret pacts and esoteric power. The recurring presence of the all-seeing eye on album covers, music videos, and stage performances serves as a visual shorthand that simultaneously celebrates and interrogates the notion of hidden influence. Such references are not deployed solely for their shock value; they function as subtle commentaries on the intersections of fame, wealth, and covert manipulation. By suggesting that extraordinary success might be intertwined with dark, enigmatic forces, these musical works critique the established power structures of the entertainment industry while engaging in a playful subversion of conventional hierarchies. In doing so, they tap into a broader cultural skepticism that questions whether the glitter of celebrity and the allure of wealth are the product of merit, chance, or an inscrutable pact with unseen powers.

Literature, too, has long found fertile ground in the myth of the Illuminati. Beyond the realms of sensational thrillers and our well-known interpretations encapsulated by popular authors, many contemporary writers employ Illuminati motifs to explore the hidden dynamics that shape human thought and societal organization. In literary works, the quest for truth is frequently depicted as an ambiguous journey, fraught with the danger of succumbing to dogmatism even as it promises liberation from ignorance. The secret society becomes an allegory for the invisible forces that govern individual identity and collective destiny, forcing readers to confront the inherent ambiguity of objective truth. Rather than offering neat solutions, these narratives reflect a deep philosophical skepticism: the search for absolute clarity may lead to intellectual homogenization, suppressing the diverse interpretations that form the backbone of a vibrant society.

Digital media has, in recent years, amplified the cultural resonance of the Illuminati myth to an unprecedented degree. The proliferation of online platforms and social networks has created spaces where the myth is continuously reinterpreted, parodied, and disseminated with astonishing speed. On these platforms, images of the all-seeing eye and other associated symbols circulate as part of the viral memetic culture, oscillating between ironic detachment and genuine conviction. However, this widespread dissemination also fosters counter-narratives and critical scrutiny, with communities actively engaging in debunking efforts, highlighting the myth's fluidity in the digital age. The digital public sphere is characterized by its echo chambers, where algorithmically curated content reinforces users' predispositions and nurtures a reflexive urge to see patterns in the ostensibly random. Here, the psychological impulse toward patternicity—the innate drive to impose order on chaotic stimuli—is vividly evident. In these digital corridors, every stray coincidence or ambiguous imagery can be woven into a narrative of hidden conspiracies, providing a sense of mastery over a world that often feels overwhelmingly complex and unpredictable.

Adding further depth to this discussion is the global dimension of the myth. Although much of the discourse about the Illuminati is dominated by Western interpretations, emerging narratives across Asia, Latin America, and Africa indicate that local adaptations are beginning to intersect with and transform the established mythos. In these regions, traditional symbols and indigenous cultural narratives are being remixed with the conventional imagery of secret societies, yielding hybrid interpretations that challenge the notion of a monolithic, Western-centric myth. These cross-cultural expressions attest to the universal appeal of the quest for hidden order, suggesting that the drive to find patterns and assign meaning to uncertainty is a reaction not confined by geographical or cultural boundaries but inherent to the human condition.

Philosophically, the modern myth of the Illuminati provokes critical inquiry into the very nature of truth and knowledge. It implicitly asks whether the Enlightenment's grand promise of universal reason, when untethered from individual autonomy, could inadvertently lead to a new form of intellectual constraint. If truth is selectively revealed through hidden power structures, one must ask whether pursuing such truth can ever be completely emancipatory. Philosophers have long debated whether a singular, all-encompassing narrative, regardless of its source, might ultimately suffocate the multifaceted nature of human experience. The myth raises the possibility that absolute clarity, far from being universally beneficial, may sometimes serve as a mechanism of control—a tool for streamlining diverse perspectives into a rigid, unyielding orthodoxy. Such inquiries invite further reflection on the delicate balance between the need for clarity and the imperative of preserving individual autonomy.

Psychologically, the enduring appeal of the Illuminati myth is deeply entwined with the human propensity for patternicity. Finding patterns provides comfort and a semblance of control in a world characterized by rapid change, overwhelming amounts of information, and a pervasive sense of uncertainty. This cognitive bias leads individuals to connect dots that may be random or unrelated—transforming fragmented pieces of data into a cohesive narrative that offers insights, however speculative, into the workings of power. The myth, therefore, not only reflects external cultural dynamics but also mirrors the internal processes of human cognition. It reminds us that our desire to impose order on chaos is as much a function of our evolutionary instincts as it is a product of historical and social influences.

In synthesizing these diverse dimensions—from the cinematic depictions in Hollywood and the lyrical expressions of popular music to the subversive narratives of modern literature and the viral spread of digital content—it becomes clear that the modern portrayal of the

Illuminati is far from static. It is a continuously evolving dialogue, reflecting our collective anxieties about the concentration of power and our persistent hope that we might attain a greater understanding of our world through the search for hidden knowledge. This myth is a living testament to the complex interplay between history, philosophy, and psychology. It encapsulates our ambivalence toward authority and our desire to decode the unseen forces shaping our lives.

Ultimately, the myth of the Illuminati endures because it is deeply interwoven with the fundamental human quest for truth amid uncertainty. It challenges us to continually question the narratives that define our understanding of power and remain vigilant against the forces that seek to simplify and control complex realities. The myth invites us to examine the illuminated promise of secret knowledge and the potential perils of enforced conformity in its manifold incarnations across film, music, literature, and digital spaces. As we navigate an interconnected world marked by rapid technological advances and shifting cultural landscapes, including the burgeoning possibilities of advanced AI and virtual realities, the enduring allure of the Illuminati reminds us that the pursuit of meaning and clarity often comes at the cost of embracing ambiguity. In this unresolved tension between order and chaos, between clarity and the suppression of diversity, lies one of the most profound challenges of our time—a challenge that impels us to seek truth not as a final destination but as an ever-evolving journey.

Chapter Sixteen

Modern-Day Conspiracies in Politics & Finance — Exploring claims about secret global control—fact vs. fiction.

In contemporary culture, the myth of the Illuminati has transformed from a narrowly defined historical phenomenon into a dynamic cultural archetype that pervades modern media and popular discourse. This reimagined symbol is no longer confined to clandestine societies of the 18th century or the treatises of Enlightenment thought; instead, it leverages those historical roots, transformed into a potent emblem of power, control, and hidden truth amid the complexities of a rapidly evolving global landscape. The myth enthralls in part because it taps into deep-seated psychological impulses—most notably, the human cognitive bias of patternicity—and partly because it serves as a canvas upon which modern anxieties about surveillance, technology, and institutional dominance are vividly painted.

The cinematic portrayals of the Illuminati have been especially influential in shaping our contemporary perceptions. Films have reconfigured the secret society into an omnipresent force that can shape historical narratives and control overarching social currents. In such works, symbols like the all-seeing eye appear repeatedly—not merely as decorative motifs but as loaded symbols that evoke divine oversight and the potential tyranny of authoritarian control. The interplay of shadow and light on the screen creates a visual tension that mirrors the conceptual duality of the myth. Here, the seductive allure of hidden knowledge is counterbalanced by the fear that such knowledge, when monopolized by an unseen elite, may suffice to quash individual autonomy. Through these cinematic narratives, viewers are invited to question whether the promise of absolute truth is worth the risk of surrendering the plurality of human experience to a single, monolithic authority.

Unlike film, popular music also deploys Illuminati symbolism as a cultural critique. Many artists, especially in genres such as hip-hop and pop, have incorporated imagery associated with secret pacts and esoteric power. The recurring presence of the all-seeing eye on album covers, music videos, and stage performances serves as a visual shorthand that simultaneously celebrates and interrogates the notion of hidden influence. Such references aren't deployed solely for shock value; they function as subtle commentaries on the intersections of fame, wealth, and covert manipulation. By suggesting that extraordinary success might be intertwined with dark, enigmatic forces, these musical works critique the established power structures of the entertainment industry while engaging in a playful subversion of conventional hierarchies. In doing so, they tap into a broader cultural skepticism that questions whether the glitter of celebrity and the allure of wealth are the product of merit, chance, or an inscrutable pact with unseen powers.

Literature, too, has long found fertile ground in the myth of the Illuminati. Beyond the realms of sensational thrillers and our well-known interpretations encapsulated by popular authors, many contemporary writers employ Illuminati motifs to explore the hidden dynamics that shape human thought and societal organization. In literary works, the quest for truth is frequently depicted as an ambiguous journey, fraught with the danger of succumbing to dogmatism even as it promises liberation from ignorance. The secret society becomes an allegory for the invisible forces that govern individual identity and collective destiny, forcing readers to confront the inherent ambiguity of objective truth. Rather than offering neat solutions, these narratives reflect a deep philosophical skepticism: the search for absolute clarity may lead to intellectual homogenization, suppressing the very diversity of interpretations that form the backbone of a vibrant society.

Digital media has, in recent years, amplified the cultural resonance of the Illuminati myth to an unprecedented degree. The proliferation of online platforms and social networks has created spaces where the myth is continuously reinterpreted, parodied, and disseminated with astonishing speed. On these platforms, images of the all-seeing eye and other associated symbols circulate as part of the viral memetic culture, oscillating between ironic detachment and genuine conviction. However, this widespread dissemination also fosters counter-narratives and critical scrutiny, with communities actively engaging in debunking efforts, highlighting the myth's fluidity in the digital age. The digital public sphere is characterized by its echo chambers, where algorithmically curated content reinforces users' predispositions and nurtures a reflexive urge to see patterns in the ostensibly random. Here, the psychological impulse toward patternicity—the innate drive to impose order on chaotic stimuli—is vividly evident. In these digital corridors, every stray coincidence or ambiguous imagery can be woven into a narrative of hidden conspiracies, providing a sense of mastery over a world that often feels overwhelmingly complex and unpredictable.

Adding further depth to this discussion is the global dimension of the myth. Although much of the discourse about the Illuminati is dominated by Western interpretations, emerging narratives across Asia, Latin America, and Africa indicate that local adaptations are beginning to intersect with and transform the established mythos. In these regions, traditional symbols and indigenous cultural narratives are being remixed with the conventional imagery of secret societies, yielding hybrid interpretations that challenge the notion of a monolithic, Western-centric myth. These cross-cultural expressions attest to the universal appeal of the quest for hidden order, suggesting that the drive to find patterns and assign meaning to uncertainty is a reaction not confined by geographical or cultural boundaries but inherent to the human condition.

Philosophically, the modern myth of the Illuminati provokes critical inquiry into the very nature of truth and knowledge. It implicitly asks whether the Enlightenment's grand promise of universal reason, when untethered from individual autonomy, could inadvertently lead to a new form of intellectual constraint. If truth is selectively revealed through hidden power structures, one must ask whether pursuing such truth can ever be completely emancipatory. Philosophers have long debated whether a singular, all-encompassing narrative, regardless of its source, might ultimately suffocate the multifaceted nature of human experience. The myth raises the possibility that absolute clarity, far from being universally beneficial, may sometimes serve as a mechanism of control—a tool for streamlining diverse perspectives into a rigid, unyielding orthodoxy. Such inquiries invite further reflection on the delicate balance between the need for clarity and the imperative of preserving individual autonomy.

Psychologically, the enduring appeal of the Illuminati myth is deeply entwined with the human propensity for patternicity—the innate cognitive tendency to find meaningful patterns in random or ambiguous data. Finding patterns provides comfort and a semblance of control in a world characterized by rapid change, overwhelming amounts of information, and a pervasive sense of uncertainty. This cognitive bias leads individuals to connect dots that may be random or unrelated—transforming fragmented pieces of data into a cohesive narrative that offers insights, however speculative, into the workings of power. The myth, therefore, not only reflects external cultural dynamics but also mirrors the internal processes of human cognition. It reminds us that our desire to impose order on chaos is as much a function of our evolutionary instincts as it is a product of historical and social influences.

In synthesizing these diverse dimensions—from the cinematic depictions in Hollywood and the lyrical expressions of popular music to the subversive narratives of modern literature and the viral spread of digital content—it becomes clear that the modern portrayal of the Illuminati is far from static. It is a continuously evolving dialogue, reflecting our collective anxieties about the concentration of power and our persistent hope that we might attain a greater understanding of our world through the search for hidden knowledge. This myth is a living testament to the complex interplay between history, philosophy, and psychology. It encapsulates our ambivalence toward authority and our desire to decode the unseen forces shaping our lives.

Ultimately, the myth of the Illuminati endures because it is deeply interwoven with the fundamental human quest for truth amid uncertainty. It challenges us to continually question the narratives that define our understanding of power and remain vigilant against the forces that seek to simplify and control complex realities. In its manifold incarnations across film, music, literature, and digital spaces, the myth invites us to examine the illuminated promise of secret knowledge and the potential perils of enforced conformity. As we navigate an interconnected world marked by rapid technological advances and shifting cultural landscapes, including the burgeoning possibilities of advanced AI and virtual realities, the enduring allure of the Illuminati reminds us that the pursuit of meaning and clarity often comes at the cost of embracing ambiguity. In this unresolved tension between order and chaos, between clarity and the suppression of diversity, lies one of the most profound challenges of our time—a challenge that impels us to seek truth not as a final destination but as an ever-evolving journey.

Chapter Seventeen

Separating Fact from Fiction – Debunking conspiracy theories vs. historical truths.

Pursuing truth in an age overflowing with competing narratives is as much an intellectual and ethical undertaking as it is a historical one. In an environment where every ambiguous symbol or half-remembered phrase can be transformed into "evidence" by the rapid churn of digital media, the challenge of separating fact from fiction takes on profound urgency. This chapter engages with that challenge by examining how conspiracy theories—especially those surrounding secret global control—emerge, persist, and can ultimately be debunked through careful historical analysis and an understanding of the psychological and digital forces at work.

At the core of these narratives lies a fundamental human impulse: the desire to impose order on chaos. When confronted with unpredictable events—a sudden economic downturn, inexplicable political upheaval, or even an oddly familiar symbol appearing in unexpected contexts—the mind seeks out patterns, weaving fragmented data into a coherent narrative. This cognitive phenomenon, sometimes called patternicity, traces its roots deep into our evolutionary past. For our ancestors, perceiving agency behind ambiguous signals was a vital survival mechanism. Today, that same predisposition often leads us to construct simplified explanations for complex events, reducing multifaceted phenomena to the machinations of an all-powerful, hidden elite. While emotionally satisfying, such shortcuts risk obscuring the nuanced interplay of factors that shape our world.

Historical records offer a compelling counterpoint to these sweeping claims. Consider the well-documented case of the Bavarian Illuminati: founded in 1776 as a slight intellectual movement committed to Enlightenment ideals, its brief existence was characterized by modest reformist ambitions rather than the elaborate, omniscient control later attributed to it by conspiracy theorists. Rigorous scholarship has demonstrated that the group's influence was limited and confined to a narrow period of political experimentation. Its eventual suppression resulted from explicit governmental opposition rather than mysterious machinations. Nevertheless, the historical facts have been reinterpreted over time, and the Illuminati's image expanded into a potent symbol—a veritable Rorschach test onto which modern anxieties about power and secrecy are projected.

The divergence between documented reality and accumulated myth is a fertile ground for cognitive bias. When historical evidence is stripped of its context and reassembled into a narrative that fits neatly into our preconceptions, the seductive allure of a single, orchestrating force becomes hard to resist. Conspiracy theories often neglect the inherent complexity of causation: historical events, whether political, economic, or cultural, are rarely the product of linear planning. Instead, they emerge from an intricate weave of influences, including individual decisions, societal trends, unforeseen accidents, and competing interests. When we fail to appreciate this complexity, it is easy to fall back upon simplified explanations that position the world as a chessboard managed by covert players.

The digital revolution has significantly influenced the spread and persistence of these oversimplified narratives. Social media platforms and algorithm-driven news feeds create environments where content is consumed and amplified without the benefit of delicate contextualization. In these digital echo chambers, isolated images, selective quotes, or out-of-context data points are repeatedly circulated until they coalesce into irrefutable evidence of a grand conspiracy. The rapid sharing of viral content transforms minor details into cornerstone "proof" for believers, while the sheer speed and volume of misinterpreted information often drown out systematic counterarguments. It makes debunking a formidable task, as belief systems, once established, are often robustly resistant to contradictory evidence, particularly when reinforced by strong emotional or social bonds. In essence, the digital landscape accelerates the spread of misinformation and entrenches cognitive biases by exposing individuals predominantly to views that reaffirm their preexisting beliefs.

Debunking such narratives, therefore, requires a dual-pronged approach. On one hand, it demands an unwavering commitment to recovering and presenting the historical record in its full complexity. By returning to primary documents, verified testimonies, and rigorous archival research, scholars can demonstrate that seemingly disparate events—like the dissolution of a small reformist group or the isolated missteps of bureaucratic institutions—do not add up to a coordinated global control scheme. A close examination of events reveals that what critics might have interpreted as secretive manipulation are, in fact, the ordinary outcomes of human endeavors: discussions held in closed rooms, the natural ebb and flow of political power, and the inevitable disorganization that accompanies revolutionary change.

On the other hand, debunking demands compassionate engagement with the underlying psychological and cultural forces that make conspiracy theories so appealing. Educators and scholars must acknowledge that the need for clarity, especially during societal stress, is genuine and pressing. It is not enough merely to catalog errors in conspiratorial narratives; one must also understand why these narratives provide comfort. When traditional institutions lose credibility—whether through demonstrable corruption, unforeseen policy failures, or simply the staggering complexity of global events—the resulting void is quickly filled by stories that promise a tidy resolution: a clear villain responsible for every misfortune. While understandable, this psychological need for closure often leads to an oversimplified understanding of events, undermining the possibility of constructive dialogue and profound reform.

Take, for example, the aftermath of the 2008 financial crisis. While detailed economic analyses point to a confluence of factors—including flawed financial instruments, regulatory failures, and widespread systemic instability—the more straightforward narrative that a hidden cabal orchestrated the collapse resonated deeply with those left reeling by economic uncertainty. Such a narrative not only offers a convenient scapegoat but also channels complex economic distress into an easily digestible storyline that divides the world into an apparent dichotomy of oppressors and the oppressed. However, looking at the multifactorial nature of financial systems, it becomes evident that no secret plot is required to explain market volatility; rather, it is the natural result of interactions in an open, competitive, and often unpredictable global economy.

Similarly, consider the portrayal of elite gatherings such as the Bilderberg meetings. Media reports and conspiracy-laden blogs often suggest that these meetings serve as clandestine sessions where world policies are decided in shadow. However, thorough investigative journalism and scholarly inquiry have consistently shown that these meetings function primarily as networking and informal discussion forums. Their private nature does not prove the existence of a hidden hand that controls global events. What happens in closed-door meetings, while not public, is not necessarily nefarious—it is part and parcel of the normal operations of political, economic, and social elites who come together to exchange ideas. When such evidence is rigorously examined, the illusion of a monolithic power structure dissolves, replaced by a more accurate representation of dispersed influence and the inherent ambiguities of decision-making in complex systems.

Philosophically, the broader challenge of separating fact from fiction in a media-saturated age also invites reconsidering what it means to know something. The Enlightenment ideal—that reason and empirical investigation can eventually illuminate truth—remains a powerful guiding principle. Nevertheless, in contemporary discourse, that ideal is constantly under siege by the realities of information manipulation and the selective presentation of facts. When powerful agencies can control or skew the flow of information, the concept of objective truth becomes slippery. This reality intensifies the ongoing crisis of trust in traditional institutions of knowledge and often targets conspiratorial narratives. This perspective does not imply that all claims of secret control are valid; instead, it suggests that selective disclosure and manipulated narratives are tools that can be, and sometimes are, employed to maintain dominance. Such a view forces us to examine the transparency structures in our governments, financial institutions, and media and to ask whether our systems are as open and accountable as they purport to be.

One must also consider the cultural dimensions of this phenomenon. Although much of the discussion surrounding conspiracies is rooted in Western historical narratives, similar impulses are evident across different cultural landscapes. In societies experiencing rapid change or crisis, the human tendency towards simplified, unifying narratives is equally potent. Local myths of concealed power and unseen manipulations often merge with global conspiracy theories, creating hybrid narratives that resonate because they speak to universally shared fears and expectations. Recognizing this cultural interplay underscores that the challenge of reconciling fact and fiction is not confined to any single context; rather, it is a global issue, reflecting the broader human condition and the universal need for meaning.

In practice, the essential work of debunking must be an ongoing process that is as much about building and sustaining a culture of critical inquiry as it is about setting the historical record straight. It involves engaging in respectful dialogue with those drawn to simplified narratives, helping them understand that complexity does not negate the possibility of genuine insight but enriches it. Empowering individuals with the tools of media literacy, critical reasoning, and historical context is crucial in an era where misinformation can spread faster than ever before. As citizens learn to question the content they encounter and the sources and mechanisms of distribution, they build a more resilient defense against the lure of conspiratorial thinking.

At its most fundamental, separating fact from fiction reaffirms our collective commitment to truth and transparency. It is a reminder that pursuing knowledge is a dynamic, ever-evolving conversation that requires us to remain alert, inquisitive, and humble in the face of complexity. Conspiracy theories, with all their seductive simplicity, are a testament to the human yearning for certainty and control. Nevertheless, as the weight of evidence shows, reality is an intricate tapestry woven from myriad threads, each contributing to a far richer and more nuanced picture than any narrative can capture.

In the end, dismantling the myth of secret global control is not about discrediting every dissenting viewpoint or asserting that all official narratives are infallible. Instead, it is about acknowledging that truth is multifaceted and that informed discourse must continuously engage with our knowledge's strengths and limitations. By encouraging a rigorous, thoughtful, and compassionate approach to understanding, we can challenge the allure of oversimplified explanations and foster a culture that prizes genuine inquiry over convenient certainties.

This ongoing endeavor to bridge the gap between fact and fiction is essential, for it underpins the integrity of our public discourse and the health of our democratic institutions. In a world where every image, quote, or data fragment can be misinterpreted when viewed in isolation, a commitment to contextual, comprehensive analysis becomes our strongest safeguard against distortion. In an accelerating information landscape, where deepfakes and advanced AI-driven disinformation campaigns pose unprecedented challenges, robust and adaptive debunking strategies are more critical than ever. As we continue to refine our understanding of both history and contemporary events, the challenge of debunking conspiracy theories remains a dynamic and vital part of our collective journey toward truth—a journey marked not by the triumph of a single narrative but by the sustained, critical engagement with the multifaceted reality that defines our shared human experience.

Chapter Eighteen
Why Secret Societies Continue to Fascinate Us – A broader look at secrecy and mystique.

In a forgotten archive of Enlightenment lore and clandestine ritual, an obscure manuscript bearing cryptic symbols beckons the curious to peer beyond the veil of everyday history. This same unyielding magnetism, the promise of hidden knowledge and secret power—has sustained the fascination with secret societies for centuries. As the final chapter of our exploration, this narrative examines why secret societies continue to captivate us today, weaving together threads of historical fact, philosophical inquiry, and psychological insight into a rich tapestry of mystique and intrigue.

At its core, the allure of secret societies lies in the timeless human quest for the unspoken and the unknown. The very idea that beneath the surface of the visible world exists a realm of hidden truths and guarded wisdom has lured kings, scholars, and commoners alike. In every generation, this notion has provided a seductive counterpoint to every day—a reminder that our understanding of power, knowledge, and identity is never complete. Instead, it is subject to constant revision and reinterpretation. These secret orders promise that what is known, however transparent it may appear, is merely the surface of a far deeper, layered reality. Such a promise is enticing, especially in an age when everyday complexity strains the limits of conventional wisdom.

Historically, secret societies have arisen from moments of cultural and political contestation. Their formation often coincided with periods when dominant institutions seemed to stifle innovation or suppress progressive ideas. From the esoteric circles of Renaissance academies to the discreet lodges of Enlightenment freethinkers, these groups served as platforms for assimilating, preserving, and challenging the established order. Far from mere conspiracies of power, many secret societies were formed as sanctuaries for intellectual dissent—a means for the marginalized to exchange revolutionary ideas away from the scrutinizing eye of authority. Even the Bavarian Illuminati, whose modest beginnings under Adam Weishaupt's guidance have been exaggerated over time, initially emerged as an experiment in social reform and Enlightenment rather than a vehicle for world domination. Over time, however, such groups were mythologized, their historical details reconfigured into a narrative that suggests an enduring and omnipresent control that defies the chaos of modern life.

This transformation from modest beginnings to mythic iconography is rooted in the interplay between memory and interpretation. History, as we know, is not merely a collection of facts but an evolving narrative sculpted by cultural perceptions and the collective imagination. The rituals, symbols, and iconography of secret societies—whether it be the all-seeing eye, the pyramid, or cryptic handshakes—have acquired a symbolic force that transcends their original purpose. They function as visual and cognitive shorthand, drawing upon deep-seated archetypes that evoke mystery and power. Even as rigorous scholarship demystifies the practical activities of these orders, the cultural imprint they have left endures, feeding a cycle in which the legend becomes more significant than the documented reality.

Psychologically, the attraction to secret societies can be understood through patternicity—a cognitive tendency to perceive patterns where none may exist or to read deliberate design into chaotic events. This mental predisposition, mildly adaptive in our evolutionary past as a survival mechanism, now predisposes us to overinterpret random coincidences as meaningful connections. Faced with the complexity of modern life—from global financial crises to rapid political shifts—the mind finds solace in attributing these events to a hidden but orderly force acting behind the scenes. In doing so, we simplify the incomprehensible. The allure of a secret cabal orchestrating history becomes a compelling narrative and a psychological balm for the anxiety that accompanies uncertainty and unpredictability.

In the modern era, digital technologies have only intensified this phenomenon. With their algorithmic curations and echo chambers, social media platforms are fertile ground for the propagation of simplified narratives. Here, isolated facts, ambiguous symbols, and out-of-context quotations are shared, remixed, and replayed until they coalesce into an unassailable body of "evidence" for secret machinations. Once a captivating idea that hints at hidden truths is released into the digital commons, it can quickly attain a self-reinforcing momentum that blurs the boundary between genuine inquiry and confirmation bias. Online communities, predisposed to seek narrative simplicity amidst a barrage of information, often embrace these ideas without the rigorous counterbalance of traditional academic scrutiny. Thus, digital media has transformed the legend of secret societies into an ever-evolving dialogue that casts fresh light on old myths and reanimates the enduring interplay between truth and perception.

Cultural dimensions further enrich this discussion. While much of the academic and popular focus has centered on Western secret societies, the fundamental allure of secrecy is a global phenomenon. Across diverse cultural landscapes—from the mystical orders of Eastern traditions to Indigenous practices that celebrate hidden realms—a recurring motif exists: the belief that the most potent truths are preserved only for those initiated into the mysteries. This cross-cultural resonance underscores a shared human longing for connection and transcendence. Whether in secret lodges, temple rituals, or sacred communal gatherings, the promise of access to a hidden world has provided communities with spiritual solace and a platform for asserting collective identity. In this sense, the persistence of secret societies in the public imagination is not merely a historical accident but a reflection of an enduring need to feel part of something larger than oneself. This belief system bridges personal and communal experiences.

Philosophically, the fascination with secret societies challenges our conventional understanding of knowledge and truth. The Enlightenment fervently championed the idea of transparency and rational inquiry, suggesting that any truth could eventually be uncovered with the right tools. Nevertheless, guarding specific knowledge—ensuring that some truths remain esoteric—implies that not all information is meant for public consumption. This very tension inspires a deep ambivalence: while the pursuit of knowledge is celebrated, there is also a recognition that some realms of understanding might forever remain elusive, perhaps even sacrosanct. Such a perspective invites us to contemplate the boundaries of informed discourse and the possibility that some mysteries, by their nature, resist definitive elucidation. The paradox of the secret society, then, is that its enduring allure lies in its simultaneous invitation to reveal and conceal—a duality that encourages us to question our assumptions about the nature of truth.

Furthermore, the narrative of secret societies often serves as a potent societal critique. In times of political disillusionment and economic instability, the recurring motif of hidden elite orchestrating events speaks to a broader skepticism regarding the legitimacy and accountability of established power structures. Even as modern institutions strive for greater transparency, public trust can wane when these institutions seem distant, bureaucratic, or unresponsive to the needs of the people. In this light, the mythic portrayal of a clandestine, all-knowing order becomes not merely an escapist fantasy but a symbolic expression of collective grievances and a call for a reexamination of power. Here, the fascination with secrecy transforms into an act of resistance—an appeal for a more nuanced understanding of who holds power and how it operates in the labyrinthine corridors of modern society.

Equally, the stories from secret societies serve as compelling narratives shaping our cultural identity. From the epic tales conveyed in ancient legends to the modern blockbusters replete with coded symbols and hidden messages, such narratives highlight the interplay between myth and memory. These stories do not solely function as escapism; they are powerful vehicles for communicating fundamental questions about authority, destiny, and the human condition. They encourage us to confront our past and present complexities, drawing on a shared heritage that is as allegorical as factual. By embracing the ambiguity inherent in any narrative of secrecy, we are reminded of the transformative power of inquiry—the idea that there might lie a glimmer of truth in every shadow, waiting to be understood on its own terms.

As we embark on the final stretch of our exploration, the digital age offers both a challenge and an opportunity to reconfigure our understanding of secret societies. While modern communication technologies endow us with unprecedented access to information, they also risk distorting that information through oversimplification, misinformation, and the seductive pull of echo chambers. Thus, the responsibility falls on us—the scholars, the inquisitive minds, and the engaged citizens—to navigate this increasingly complex landscape with skepticism and imagination. By critically engaging with these narratives, questioning the apparent certainties, and embracing the beauty of complexity, we can hope to reconcile the dual impulses of rational inquiry and mythic wonder.

In the final analysis, the profound fascination with secret societies endures because it encapsulates one of the most essential aspects of "the Human Experience": the quest for meaning amid uncertainty. Whether driven by a desire to access forbidden wisdom, to assert a sense of identity against an impersonal modern order, or to search for the hidden patterns that underlie existence, our attraction to secrecy reflects the multifaceted nature of our very being. It is an interplay between our yearning for clarity and our acceptance of mystery A dynamic tension that challenges and enriches our understanding of the world.

As this exploration draws to a close, we are reminded that our journey toward truth is an ongoing dialogue that spans generations, cultures, and disciplines. The enduring mystique of secret societies stands as a testament not to the evasion of truth but to the complexity of truth itself. In a world characterized by rapid change and perennial uncertainty, the allure of hidden knowledge remains a beacon, inviting us to look beyond the surface and appreciate the infinite layers of meaning woven into the fabric of reality.

In the quiet after word of this long voyage through hidden histories and esoteric narratives, we find a final invitation: to remain ever curious, ever-questioning, and ever open to the profound possibility that, within every secret, there lies not only mystery and intrigue but also the potential for deeper understanding. Though the pages of this book now end, its insights continue to echo a call to embrace the complexity of our collective existence and to pursue truth with the courage and humility that such a quest demands.

Epilogue

The Eternal Shadow of the Illuminati.

As history fades into legend, the Illuminati remain—a name whispered in speculation, embedded in pop culture, and debated in the corridors of conspiracy. Their origins were simple: a society dedicated to enlightenment, reason, and intellectual pursuit. Their downfall was swift, crushed beneath the weight of political fear and suspicion. And yet, their presence lingers in the modern imagination, evolving far beyond their historical reality.

What began as a modest secret society in 18th-century Bavaria has become the phantom of power narratives—a group accused of manipulating events, influencing governments, and orchestrating a hidden world order. But are such claims grounded in evidence, or do they merely reflect humanity's deep-seated need to explain chaos through unseen forces?

Throughout history, people have sought explanations for the unexplainable, weaving intricate tales of hidden puppet masters controlling the fate of nations. The Illuminati, whether real or imagined, fit neatly into this tradition. In times of political turmoil, economic instability, and shifting social structures, their supposed influence provides a convenient answer to uncomfortable questions. If power seems distant and decisions are made beyond public reach, the idea of an elite, unseen force offers a compelling alternative to mundane reality.

Yet as centuries pass, their story has transformed. The Illuminati of Weishaupt's era were intellectuals, revolutionaries, and advocates for reason. The Illuminati of today are the subject of countless theories, evolving into something far greater—and far less tangible—than their original incarnation. The age of the printing press whispered their downfall, but the age of digital media has ensured their survival. A name once associated with Enlightenment ideals is now linked to coded symbolism, secret societies, and fears of global control. Whether in music videos, political discourse, or blockbuster films, they remain a presence—a shadow cast over culture itself.

What does this say about humanity? Perhaps the legacy of the Illuminati is not about their actions, but about our enduring fascination with secrecy. In an era where information is limitless yet trust is scarce, the allure of unseen forces directing the world persists. Governments rise and fall, economies fluctuate, but conspiracy thrives. And as long as the unknown remains, so will whispers of the Illuminati.

So where does the truth begin and fiction end? The answer is unclear, and perhaps it always will be. The Illuminati are no longer merely a historical entity; they are an idea, a mythology—one that continues to evolve. Their existence may have been brief, but their legend is eternal.

The question is no longer whether they are real, but why we want them to be!

Bibliography

Chapter One

Elizabeth Eisenstein

• The Printing Revolution in Early Modern Europe — Analyzes the profound impact of the printing press on the dissemination of knowledge, literacy, and cultural transformation.

Hugh Trevor-Roper

• Europe and the Making of Modernity, 1648–1815 — Provides a detailed account of the political and cultural shifts that laid the groundwork for modern Europe.

Geoffrey Parker

• The Thirty Years' War — A seminal discussion discussing the devastating conflict that reshaped Europe and influenced later Enlightenment and political thought.

C.V. Wedgwood

• The Thirty Years' War — A classic narrative that offers insights into one of Europe's most significant conflicts and its long-term effects on societal structures.

Peter H. Wilson

• Europe's Tragedy: A New History of the Thirty Years War — Presents a modern reinterpretation of the war's impact on the evolution of European politics and the emerging state system.

Note: much of this book comes from these sources. Summaries only given now

Chapter Two

Primary Philosophical and Political Texts (Direct Sources)

• What is Enlightenment? by Immanuel Kant (1784) — Kant's seminal essay, in which he famously urges "Sapere aude!" ("Dare to know!"), remains one of the foundational texts of Enlightenment thought.

• The Social Contract by Jean Jacques Rousseau (1762) — Rousseau's treatise on the nature of political legitimacy and collective will provides key insight into ideas of equality and direct democracy.

• The Spirit of the Laws by Montesquieu (1748) — This work introduces the concept of separation of powers, influencing modern political structures and offering a template for limiting authority.

• Novum Organum by Francis Bacon (1620) — Bacon's work champions the experimental method and empirical inquiry, which played a crucial role in shaping Enlightenment approaches to science and reason.

• Meditations on First Philosophy by René Descartes (1641) — Descartes' exploration of doubt and rationalism laid important philosophical groundwork for challenging accepted truths.

• Candide by Voltaire (1759) — Although this is a satirical novella, its incisive critique of established institutions and dogma vividly illustrates Enlightenment ideals in literary form.

Enlightenment Historians and Comprehensive Overviews

• The Enlightenment: An Interpretation by Peter Gay (1966–1969) — Gay's extensive work offers a sweeping interpretation of how Enlightenment thought reshaped society, providing context for the intellectual currents that later influenced groups like the Illuminati.

• Radical Enlightenment: Philosophy and the Making of Modernity, 1650–1750 by Jonathan Israel (2001) — Israel examines the more radical currents of thought that underpinned modern political ideas, deepening our understanding of the ideological environment that gave rise to secret societies.

• The Business of Enlightenment: A Publishing History of the Encyclopédie, 1775–1800 by Robert Darnton (1988) — Darnton's work links the spread of Enlightenment ideas to the revolutionary impact of print culture, emphasizing how ideas were disseminated and institutionalized.

Works on Salon Culture and the Republic of Letters

• Articles and studies on Parisian salons (such as those found in works by Dena Goodman and related scholarly articles) — These sources explore how salons served as incubators for debate and intellectual exchange, vital in propagating Enlightenment ideas across social boundaries.

• Enlightenment Salons: The Convergence of Female and Philosophic Ambitions (JSTOR article by Dena Goodman or similar) — This scholarly work investigates the role of salons in bringing together diverse thinkers and in forming the communal backdrop from which secret societies later emerged.

Historical Investigations into Secret Societies and the Illuminati
Elizabeth Eisenstein

The Printing Revolution in Early Modern Europe — Eisenstein's groundbreaking study discusses the transformative impact of the printing press on European society and how technology facilitated the spread of Enlightenment ideas and radical critiques of tradition.

Hugh Trevor-Roper

• Europe and the Making of Modernity, 1648–1815 — A broad historical account that situates the Enlightenment within the larger context of European political and cultural change following the Peace of Westphalia. His work helps explain the environment that allowed secret societies to emerge.

Margaret C. Jacob

• Various works, including discussions in articles and essays) — Jacob has contributed extensively to the scholarship on Freemasonry and its role in the Enlightenment. Her research investigates how Masonic networks influenced political and scientific discourse across Europe.

Arthur Herman

• The Scottish Enlightenment: The Scot's Invention of the Modern World — Though focused on the Scottish context, Herman's work provides valuable insights into how Enlightenment ideas were not only European-wide but also fostered unique national reforms that influenced secret associative practices.

Chapter Three

Encyclopædia Britannica – "Illuminati" and "What was the Bavarian illuminati group?" Provides a scholarly overview of the Bavarian

Illuminati's origins, goals, and the ideological context of late Enlightenment Europe. • Discusses the founder's intention to replace religious domination with a "religion of reason" and offers insight into how Weishaupt's ideas aligned with contemporary intellectual currents.

All That's Interesting – "Adam Weishaupt, The Man Who Founded The Illuminati" • A popular history article summarizing Weishaupt's life, his motivations for founding the Illuminati, and the spread of his ideas. • Includes accessible explanations of the organization's original name, structure, and its evolution—with attention to how Enlightenment thought was integral to Weishaupt's vision.

Royal Art Society – "The Original 1776 Bavarian Illuminatenordes: The Order of the Illuminati, Part I" • Offers a focused historical narrative of the founding of the order, including its early members, organizational structure, and influences drawn from Freemasonry and Jesuit models. • Provides specific details on how Weishaupt modeled the order's hierarchical system and initiated its secretive practices.

EBSCO Research Starters – Illuminati Topic Package • Presents a curated set of scholarly articles and reference entries discussing the formation of the Illuminati, its goals, and broader socio-political context in 18th-century Bavaria. • Useful for academic perspectives on the organization's internal methods (such as rank divisions and secret rituals) and its gradual suppression by the Bavarian authorities.

Academia.edu – "The Bavarian Illuminati: A Brief Historical Context" • Features research papers that analyze the origins and ideological backdrop of the Illuminati in light of the broader rationalist currents of the Late Enlightenment. • Provides insights into Weishaupt's motivations, his struggle for academic freedom, and how his early experiences at Ingolstadt contributed to his anti-clerical and reformist agenda.

Chapter Four
Jessica Pearce Rotondi – Has written about secret societies, including the Illuminati and Freemasons, in historical contexts
Chapter Five
• Hermann Schüttler – Die Mitglieder des Illuminatenordens 1776–1787/93
• Reinhard Markner – Die Illuminaten: Aufklärung, Geheimnis, Revolution
• Monika Neugebauer-Wölk – Illuminaten und Freimaurer: Studien zur Aufklärung
• Richard van Dülmen – Die Gesellschaft der Aufklärung: Zur bayerischen Illuminatenbewegung
• Tobias Daniels – Die Illuminaten und ihre Netzwerke
Chapter Six
• Mark Dice – The Illuminati: Facts & Fiction
• David Livingstone – Terrorism and the Illuminati: A Three Thousand Year History
• Arthur Goldwag – Cults, Conspiracies, and Secret Societies
• Jim Marrs – Rule by Secrecy: The Hidden History that Connects the Trilateral Commission, the Freemasons & the Great Pyramids

• Charles River Editors – The Illuminati: The History of One of the World's Most Notorious Secret Societies
Chapter Seven

• René Le Forestier – The Bavarian Illuminati: The Rise and Fall of the World's Most Secret Society

• Jon E. Graham – The Bavarian Illuminati

• Vernon Stauffer – New England and the Bavarian Illuminati (1918)

• Ethan Harrison – Memoirs of a Bavarian Illuminati Hunter III
Chapter Eight

• John Robison – Proofs of a Conspiracy Against All the Religions and Governments of Europe

• Augustin Barruel – Memoirs Illustrating the History of Jacobinism

• Una Birch – Secret Societies: Illuminati, Freemasons, and the French Revolution

• Nicholas Bonneville – Illuminati Manifesto of World Revolution (1792): L'Esprit des Religions
Chapter Nine

• René Le Forestier – The Bavarian Illuminati

• Augustin Barruel – Memoirs Illustrating the History of Jacobinism

• John Robison – Proofs of a Conspiracy Against All the Religions and Governments of Europe

• Brian Desborough – They Cast No Shadows: A Collection of Essays on the Illuminati, Revisionist History, and Suppressed Technologies

Chapter Ten

• Abbé Augustin Barruel – Memoirs Illustrating the History of Jacobinism

• John Robison – Proofs of a Conspiracy

Chapter Eleven

• John Robison – Proofs of a Conspiracy Against All the Religions and Governments of Europe

• Augustin Barruel – Memoirs Illustrating the History of Jacobinism

• James H. Billington – Fire in the Minds of Men: Origins of the Revolutionary Faith

• Terry Melanson – Perfectibilists: The 18th Century Bavarian Order of the Illuminati

• Reinhard Markner & Hermann Schüttler – Correspondence of the Illuminati

• Dr. Olaf Simons – FactGrid: Illuminati Research Database

• Michael Taylor – The French Revolution as Illuminati Conspiracy

• Jean Baptiste Simonini – Simonini's Letter: The 19th Century Text That Influenced Antisemitic Conspiracy Theories About the Illuminati

Chapter Twelve

• Albert L. Weeks – Myths of the Cold War: Amending Historiographic Distortions

• Richard Raack – Stalin's Drive to the West: 1938-1945, The Origins of the Cold War

• Doctor Paradox – The Illuminati - Conspiracy Theories Dictionary

• David Aaronovitch – Voodoo Histories: The Role of the Conspiracy Theory in Shaping Modern History

• Mark Fenster – Conspiracy Theories: Secrecy and Power in American Culture

• Michael Barkun – A Culture of Conspiracy: Apocalyptic Visions in Contemporary America

• Robert Alan Goldberg – Enemies Within: The Culture of Conspiracy in Modern America

• Nicholas Hagger – The Secret History of the West: The Influence of Secret Organizations on Western History

• Jim Marrs – Rule by Secrecy: The Hidden History That Connects the Trilateral Commission, the Freemasons, and the Great Pyramids

Chapter Thirteen

• Nicholas Goodrick-Clarke – The Occult Roots of Nazism

• Richard Cavendish – The History of Magic

• Antoine Faivre – Access to Western Esotericism

• Wouter Hanegraaff – Esotericism and the Academy: Rejected Knowledge in Western Culture

• Mircea Eliade – A History of Religious Ideas

• Peter Levenda – Unholy Alliance: A History of Nazi Involvement with the Occult

• Owen Davies – Grimoires: A History of Magic Books

• Colin Wilson – Illuminations: A Journey Through the Eternal Now

Chapter Fourteen

- Nicholas Goodrick-Clarke – The Occult Roots of Nazism
- Richard Cavendish – The History of Magic
- Antoine Faivre – Access to Western Esotericism
- Wouter Hanegraaff – Esotericism and the Academy: Rejected Knowledge in Western Culture
- Mircea Eliade – A History of Religious Ideas
- Peter Levenda – Unholy Alliance: A History of Nazi Involvement with the Occult
- Owen Davies – Grimoires: A History of Magic Books
- Colin Wilson – Illuminations: A Journey Through the Eternal Now

illuminati in movies source

- The 26 Best Movies About The Illuminati & Other Secret Societies (Ranker) – https://www.ranker.com/list/movies-about-secret-societies/harper-brooks
- The 20 Best Illuminati Movies (IMDb) – https://www.imdb.com/list/ls052522802/
- "Illuminati" Movies – The Movie Database (TMDB) – https://www.themoviedb.org/keyword/5960-illuminati/movie

Chapter Fifteen

- Nicholas Goodrick Clarke – The Occult Roots of Nazism
- Richard Cavendish – The History of Magic
- Wouter Hanegraaff – Esotericism and the Academy: Rejected Knowledge in Western Culture
- Peter A. Levenda – Unholy Alliance: A History of Nazi Involvement with the Occult

• Joseph E. Uscinski – American Conspiracy Theories

• Gary Lachman – Turn Off Your Mind: The Mystical Dimensions of Music and Its Hidden History

Chapter Sixteen

• Nicholas Goodrick Clarke – The Occult Roots of Nazism

• Richard Cavendish – The History of Magic

• Wouter Hanegraaff – Esotericism and the Academy: Rejected Knowledge in Western Culture

• Peter A. Levenda – Unholy Alliance: A History of Nazi Involvement with the Occult

• Joseph E. Uscinski – American Conspiracy Theories

• Gary Lachman – Turn Off Your Mind: The Mystical Dimensions of Music and Its Hidden History

Chapter Seventeen

• Joseph E. Uscinski – American Conspiracy Theories

• Richard Hofstadter – The Paranoid Style in American Politics

• Michael Barkun – A Culture of Conspiracy: Apocalyptic Visions in Contemporary America

• Nicholas Goodrick Clarke – The Occult Roots of Nazism

• Richard Cavendish – The History of Magic

• Wouter Hanegraaff – Esotericism and the Academy: Rejected Knowledge in Western Culture

• Peter A. Levenda – Unholy Alliance: A History of Nazi Involvement with the Occult

• Gary Lachman – Turn Off Your Mind: The Mystical Dimensions of Music and Its Hidden History

Chapter Eighteen

- Andrew Watkins – The Illuminati: The History And Truth Behind The Illuminati
- Charles River Editors – The Illuminati: The History of One of the World's Most Notorious Secret Societies
- Mark Dice – The Illuminati: Facts & Fiction
- David Livingstone – Terrorism and the Illuminati: A Three Thousand Year History
- Jim Marrs – Rule by Secrecy: The Hidden History that Connects the Trilateral Commission, the Freemasons & the Great Pyramids
- Arthur Goldwag – Cults, Conspiracies, and Secret Societies: The Straight Scoop on Freemasons, The Illuminati, Skull and Bones, Black Helicopters, The New World Order, and many, many more

Index